OVERVIEW

Overview

Organizations have always had the capacity to evolve. However, today they need to evolve even more quickly and intelligently to sustain their competitive advantage. Market conditions and customer demands are constantly changing, and if organizations can anticipate and make the most of new opportunities, they'll be more likely to survive and prosper in the future. In a dynamic business environment, organizational leaders must make learning a cornerstone of their organization's culture.

So how can you tell if your organization is adequately prepared to meet such rapidly changing demands? In this course you'll learn how to assess the strength of your organization's learning culture. First, you'll find out what organizational learning really is, and how it encompasses much more than traditional "training."

You'll discover how training, knowledge management, and technology are all critical tools that support an organization's ability to learn. Organizations also need the key elements of a learning culture: holistic thinking, integrated learning opportunities, a capacity for change and improvement, a focus on collaboration, and personal commitment from employees. It's in evaluating these key elements that you'll learn how to assess the strength of your own organization's learning culture.

*

If learning is so beneficial, why do some people have difficulty? The answer lies partly in workplace distractions. The demands on people's time and the speed of events make it difficult for them to recognize and assimilate new information.

Organizations that want to adapt to changing business environments need to foster a learning culture. Even the best training environment won't enable learning if people don't take the time to process information and learn. A learning culture reflects the organizational beliefs and practices that encourage continuous development. People who work in such a culture embrace continuous self-development and seek to learn and grow.

There are obstacles to learning that you, as a manager and leader, need to overcome. Some organizational structures and cultures present obstacles such as hierarchical thinking and isolation. Hierarchical thinking – where leaders are the thinkers and employees are the doers – stifles learning by making nonmanagers feel their ideas aren't valued. Isolation limits interaction between people who have different perspectives, thus limiting their opportunity to learn.

This course will provide tools for overcoming these obstacles and for creating five key conditions that allow a learning culture to flourish. Consider the first four conditions:

- the freedom to explore others' thoughts, opinions, and actions,
- a habit of reflection, inquiry, and objectivity,
- egalitarian relationships that promote power sharing and responsibility at all levels, and
- collaborative practices that encourage people to share information and learning experiences.

The fifth and most important condition supporting a learning culture is motivation for learning and growth. Motivation is important because organizational learning is mostly self-directed. This means that people take responsibility for their own learning. Motivated employees are more creative and they're more committed to learning and being productive. Establishing these conditions will help to promote a learning culture in your organization.

**

In the rapidly changing business environments of the 21st century, trends emerge and pass in a matter of months. New markets open and prosper while traditional markets stagnate. For companies to survive in this world they must be prepared to change and adapt to keep up with their competitors. Companies increasingly turn to organizational learning to remain competitive.

Organizational learning represents a commitment from an organization to develop the intellectual and productive capabilities of its workforce. It's a process that continuously searches for opportunities to introduce improvement measures throughout an organization. In today's business environment, the company with the best workforce usually prevails. This is why more companies are making the necessary changes to become learning organizations.

A learning organization encourages continuous learning for all employees, as well as the open exchange of knowledge and information across all levels. This course introduces four practices that learning organizations typically have in place: planning for learning, building knowledge, diffusing knowledge, and applying knowledge.

This course will provide information on practices that support learning initiatives and can help you create a learning culture in your own organization. Ways in which you can plan for learning will be introduced, including conducting a learning needs assessment. You will also examine ways to acquire existing knowledge and create new knowledge. Finally, you'll learn how to diffuse and apply this knowledge throughout your organization.

***

What might many successful organizations have in common? Chances are, they're built on learning cultures. Through continuous learning and agility, these organizations can continue to flourish. Once its been built, sustaining a learning culture is key to an organization's ongoing success.

Sustaining a learning culture isn't a simple matter. Any learning activity – be it a training program, event, or initiative of any kind – must justify its existence. To justify the time and money spent on these activities, it's important to make sure they achieve the stated goals. Every learning experience must have a beneficial impact on the participants and the organization.

In order to ensure that a learning culture is sustained, it's vital to evaluate the success of learning activities. Evaluation plays a pivotal role in proving that a learning culture delivers results. It brings to light whether participants in learning activities are gaining knowledge and improving performance. It calculates the impact of learning on the organization as a whole. The evaluation process also helps answer whether organizations are getting a return on investment from learning activities.

Organizations that properly evaluate learning and sustain a learning culture are at an advantage. As they continue to learn, they continue to improve, as do their chances of success. This course looks at sustaining the momentum of learning by fostering a learning culture. You'll also find out how learning impacts the individual and the organization.

CHAPTER ONE
Fundamentals of Organizational Learning

Learning

The process of learning is sometimes underestimated – it's so much more than just the communication of information. Consider Sam, a mathematically gifted college student attending a one-hour lecture on civil engineering. His lecturer outlines the mechanical equations required to design a bridge. Sam takes notes diligently. The lecturer then gives an assignment to design and construct a model footbridge. Do you think Sam has now learned enough to design and build his own bridge? It's unlikely.

Learning takes time, understanding, and experience. Many people think of learning as the acquisition of knowledge, something achieved in the classroom – as in Sam's case. It's true that learning can be defined as a positive change in knowledge and skills. However, learning also applies to changes in attitudes and behavior gained from experience.

Learning can play a central role in organizations. A positive learning culture can motivate and energize employees to focus on the organization's strategic objectives. Organizations therefore need to be committed to learning in order to prosper.

By definition, learning is a process that results in long-term change. When people learn, they adopt new ways of perceiving and acting on the world around them.

A permanent change in the attitudes and behaviors of employees will go beyond the acquisition of knowledge; it'll positively influence the culture of the organization.

You may have noted that people learn from training courses or from observation. People also learn from past experiences – for example learning to complete a task from trial and error. This is known as adapting. People can learn from envisioning different future outcomes and acting on that vision. This is known as preparing. Another form of learning is developing. In this case, people are learning about the present, building on existing knowledge and developing their understanding based on new information.

Question

Reconsider Sam's situation. He's the college student learning to design and construct a bridge. Match.

Sam's activities to the type of learning they represent.

Options:

A. Sam tries to build a model bridge to see if it remains erect

B. Sam determines what he requires from his bridge, and anticipates design pitfalls he needs to avoid

C. Sam studies a modern bridge under construction

Targets:

1. Adapting
2. Preparing
3. Developing

Answer:

The process of trial and error is an example of learning through adapting.

Envisioning future requirements and pitfalls is an example of learning through preparing.

Learning about the present and building on existing knowledge is an example of learning through developing.

Organizational learning

Learning theorists have outlined a number of principles about how adults learn in organizational contexts:
- adults tend to be pragmatic and learn only what's relevant to perform their job well,
- they approach learning with a unique set of preferences – for example, some favor hands-on learning, while others prefer listening or observing,
- they usually like to be in control of their own learning,
- adults like to progress at their own pace, and,
- in most cases, adult learning is effective while on the job and in social settings.

There are three distinct levels of learning in organizations: the individual level, the group level, and the organizational level. The three learning levels are linked in that learning must be effective at all levels for an organization to be a successful learning organization.

Developing a Culture of Learning

See each learning level to learn more about it.

The individual level

Learning at the individual level occurs when a person acquires a skill, gains knowledge, or achieves a change in attitude or behavior. It can happen through a number of channels, including self-study, research, or observation. For example, an employee in a bank might learn the computer system, how to process payments, and customer service etiquette by completing an e-learning course, reading procedures, and observing a colleague.

The group level

Learning at the group level is the acquisition of knowledge, skills, and competencies within a group. For example, an orientation session about personality styles helps members of a team relate more effectively to each other.

The organizational level

Learning at the organizational level represents the collective intellect and productive capability of employees. It's achieved through commitment to continuous improvement across the organization. Continuous improvement is the ability to improve people's capacity to change and evolve – in other words, "getting better at getting better."

For example, an organization might have a solution-focused culture where all employees abstain from blame during a crisis and instead learn to actively seek solutions.

For an organization to be deemed a "learning organization," it must be proactive, not reactive. It must anticipate and prepare for external opportunities and events. The key to success is encouraging and providing opportunities for continuous learning. Ideas, processes, and attitudes must adapt to the needs of customers and the market.

Organizational learning influences an organization's culture. A culture of continuous reviews and improvement is more desirable than a defensive culture. A learning culture doesn't focus on blame or find comfort in outdated practices.

In order to create a learning culture, an organization's leaders need to ensure that employees at all levels have a positive attitude toward learning. It must start at the top – with the leaders – and filter down throughout the organization. Everyone must be aware of and enthusiastically accept responsibility for being a learner. There must be a culture of respect, active listening, and effective communication.

Question

Which description best defines organizational learning?

Options:

1. Continuous improvement through leveraging the collective intelligence and productivity of committed employees

2. Defining the optimal intellectual and productive capacity of an organization and committing to that capacity for the long term

3. Commitment to ensuring each employee is aware of and enthusiastically accepts responsibility for being a learner

Answer:

Option 1: This is the correct option. Continuous improvement is the key to organizational learning. An organization must constantly evolve its intellectual and productive capacity.

Option 2: This option is incorrect. The optimal intellect and productive capacity of an organization will change in the long run. A learning organization must be adaptive through continuous improvement.

Option 3: This option is incorrect. Each employee's awareness and acceptance is an important step in achieving a learning organization. However, key components of organizational learning include continuous improvement in intellect and productivity.

Value of organizational learning

Now consider Scott, a CEO of a kitchen appliance company. He wants his organization to survive and succeed. He knows that his organization's response to its ever-changing environment is critical to its success or failure. Organizational learning can help Scott's organization deal with globalization, technological change, and customer influences. To succeed, his management team must be smart and adapt quickly. To achieve this, they consider learning a cornerstone of organizational strategy for survival and growth.

Globalization has brought Scott's investors, competitors, and people of various cultures closer than before. The organization has had to seek a better understanding of global markets, different cultural values and needs, product offerings, and local trends.

Scott knows that in today's marketplace the consumer has a louder voice. His customers have the power to shop worldwide. They can shop online to find the most innovative, low cost, quality appliances with the best standards of service, and have them delivered right to their doors. As the demands of consumers evolve, Scott's organization is continuously learning to meet these ever-changing needs.

Technology has also revolutionized the global marketplace for Scott. For example, new technologies have made the company's products smaller and more user-friendly to more consumers. As technology advances, Scott also makes sure that the organization uses technology to enhance learning for employees.

As well as helping organizations deal with business imperatives, organizational learning brings many other benefits. These include enhanced agility, greater commitment, improved performance, and a positive reputation.

See each benefit in order to learn more.

Enhanced agility

Organizational learning enables organizations to respond more rapidly to changes. Organizations achieve this by encouraging a culture of continuous improvement, of looking for opportunities and being ready to seize them. They must improve their ability to improve.

For example, managers continuously review procedures and processes to find better ways to do things. Or perhaps, a leader anticipates the changing skill set of her team and implements a succession plan.

Greater commitment

Organizational learning contributes to greater commitment from employees. Employees will be motivated and energized by a continuously evolving organization, and by learning life skills such as problem solving and critical thinking. Satisfied, energized employees are usually committed and productive. Leaders, too, can gain satisfaction from watching employees develop, grow, and evolve with the organization.

Improved performance

Along with greater commitment comes better performance. When employees are motivated and committed to improving, processes become more efficient, and the quality of products and services can improve significantly.

In order to ensure this is a continuous benefit to the organization, leaders in top learning organizations establish robust performance review processes that reward improvement. They strive to develop competencies for employees at all levels in the organization.

Positive reputation

With a commitment to improvement, an organization can rise to the top of its industry and gain the reputation of a market leader for its innovative products or superior customer service.

Organizations that demonstrate a commitment to learning will also gain a good reputation among potential employees – attracting the best and brightest. This is because talented and committed people will be drawn to a positive learning environment.

These benefits of organizational learning are all interrelated. And together they can have a positive effect on an organization's competitive advantage and growth potential.

Question

Developing a Culture of Learning

Why should leaders focus their attention on organizational learning?
Options:
1. It helps organizations maintain a good name in a global marketplace
2. It helps organizations keep up with technology and innovation in a competitive marketplace
3. It helps leaders improve employee efficiency and productivity
4. It helps leaders control what is learned by employees
5. It helps streamline the performance management process
6. It helps organizations strengthen employee commitment

Answer:
Option 1: This option is correct. Organizational learning is central to improving a company's reputation in a global marketplace with customers and potential employees.

Option 2: This option is correct. Organizational learning can give an organization's leaders the agility to respond quickly to technological advances and changes in the marketplace.

Option 3: This option is correct. Organizational learning means continuously reviewing procedures and processes to make them more efficient. It can also increase commitment and productivity in employees.

Option 4: This option is incorrect. Control over employees isn't the cornerstone of organizational learning. Leaders should promote continuous agility and adaptability to change.

Option 5: This option is incorrect. A focus on organizational learning doesn't necessarily make the performance management process any simpler.

Option 6: This option is correct. Organizational learning encourages motivation and commitment in employees. They'll be motivated by learning life skills such as problem solving and critical thinking.

Training versus learning

Classroom-based training, online courses, and on-the-job training are standard learning opportunities in most large organizations. But it's not so easy to define what makes an organization a successful learning organization. Some people think training is sufficient. But although training is an essential ingredient, being a learning organization involves much more than that.

You likely noted some formalized means of passing on information, such as classroom-based training or e-learning. These are modes of training. Many organizations consider training and learning to be synonymous, but there are important differences. In fact, the concept of learning is much broader than training.

First, consider training. Training is instruction embedded in the workplace that's focused on teaching specific work-related skills and knowledge. Typically, the goal of training is to help employees perform the job-related skills or competencies they need in their daily job functions or to meet other types of organizational requirements. Training is typically structured into formal learning events, like classroom-based workshops or e-learning courses, and participation is usually externally driven by someone other than the learner. For example, a company may create a training program to teach employees how to use a new computer system.

See each characteristic of training to learn more about it.

Focused and specific

Training is focused on teaching skills and knowledge related to specific organizational or business requirements. Workplace training usually has very specific goals for improving performance. It can be used to teach new behaviors as well as to enhance existing skills.

Examples of training courses range from technical courses such as web page development, to behavioral courses, such as communication skills.

Job-related

Training is purposeful teaching or imparting of information conducted at, or made available in, the workplace. As such, the goal of training is usually focused on improving critical job-related competencies, such as managing technical operations, using project management tools, demonstrating product features and functions, and practicing good management techniques. These skills may or may not be transferable to other job responsibilities.

Structured and formal

Most training is highly structured in terms of learning objectives, learning time, or learning support, and organized into training events associated with formal learning. The purpose of a structured approach is to deliver consistent, efficient, and effective performance improvement across one or more groups of employees. Formal learning is intentional. Training is, therefore, planned and intentional.

Common examples of structured training events include formal courses such as instructor-led training, e-learning courses, hands-on labs, lectures, and workshops. Other approaches, like shadowing, may be less formal but still require an overall structure to achieve the desired training outcomes.

Externally driven

The need for workplace training is almost always driven by company, organization, or job-related factors that are external to the individual employees. New-hire and on boarding programs are good examples because it's obvious that these programs cover company-specific rules, policies, and procedures (vacation policy, how to use the internal expense system, e-mail protocol, etc.) that employees usually don't need or use outside of their work environment.

Learning, on the other hand, is the ongoing act of acquiring new or modifying existing knowledge, behaviors, skills, values, or preferences. The opportunities for learning are unlimited because they occur from the day we are born as part of our everyday lives as well as part of our professional lives. Learning can occur anytime and anywhere, intentionally or unintentionally, consciously or unconsciously, and with or without connection to job requirements or formal instructional or training materials. Learning is therefore a much more personal and self-motivated experience than training alone.

See each characteristic of learning to learn more about it.

Ongoing and unlimited

The saying "You learn something new every day" is uttered by young and old alike when they learn or realize something new for the first time. Keeping in mind that learning is the act of acquiring new or modifying existing skills and knowledge, it's easy to see that the opportunities for learning are ongoing and unlimited. In fact, this is a major differentiator for how people think about training and learning. Training typically has a well-defined work-related focus and associated performance outcomes that mark an end point. In contrast, learning started in any circumstance, including training, can be applied and continue without any limits to time, place, or context.

For example, learning negotiation skills as part of a company-provided training program can help a client services manager win new contracts in various situations on the job, and it can also help him get a better price when purchasing a new home. Conversely, a personally initiated research project on how to get the best price when buying a new home could also help an operations manager get a better price on a building or property he's purchasing for his company.

Anytime, anywhere

The anytime, anywhere nature of learning means it's inclusive of all circumstances, including training. So although training doesn't guarantee learning, it is one of the many ways in which learning can and does occur. But the concept of learning is much broader and allows for formal and informal, structured and unstructured, intentional and unintentional – even accidental – learning. It also encompasses skills and knowledge that most people consider applicable across both work and personal life situations. Structured, formal, and intentional learning is familiar and accepted. It's more difficult to understand and take advantage of the fact that learning can be unintentional, even accidental.

Self-motivated

The anytime, anywhere nature of learning means it's up to individual learners to motivate themselves to actively choose from and engage in the many learning opportunities they encounter each day. Learning is an active process that requires individual commitment, personal responsibility, and self-direction to sustain. Therefore ongoing learning is motivated much more by personal, internal factors than external factors. Embracing and capitalizing on the full range of learning opportunities is what self-directed, life-long learning is all about.

Training is an important activity when it's used to support learning. In other words, when you embark on training, learning should be the intended outcome or goal.

Organizations can adapt their training programs to optimize the learning process. This involves a dynamic combination of training in tactical skills, plus longer-term development tailored to the individual who is learning. It also involves encouraging people to take ownership of their own learning process.

Many organizations are making an effort to personalize training experiences in order to facilitate learning. For example, instead of lecturing on information, the facilitator draws on the required theory, and enables learners to accept the information by connecting it to their day-to-day activities.

Question

Match the descriptions to the appropriate type of activity (Learning or Training). Each activity may match to more than one description.

Options:

A. Focused on job-related competencies
B. Structured to be consistent and efficient
C. Applied and continued without limits to time, place, or context
D. Motivated by personal and internal factors
E. Can occur anytime or anywhere

Targets:

1. Training
2. Learning

Knowledge management and technology

Training is one activity that can support learning. Knowledge management is another. Drawing from many disciplines, including information management and networking, knowledge management involves sourcing, developing, and using knowledge that's important to the organization. Knowledge management is necessary to support learning, but it's not sufficient on its own.

Knowledge management in organizations is primarily concerned with knowledge – not data or information. Data is raw material, and information is a collection of this raw material.

Knowledge is the interpretation of information. Successful interpretation of information requires the learner to draw meaning and make connections that are useful to the organization.

Knowledge management is the productive use of knowledge to maximize benefit to the organization.

Effective knowledge management must ensure that information is available and accessible to all employees. Knowledge management must therefore include several important activities: the acquisition, development, retention, and distribution of knowledge.

See each activity to learn more.

Acquisition

Knowledge acquisition is sourcing external knowledge and integrating it into the organization's library of knowledge. For example, relationships with customers, suppliers, competitors, and partners have the potential to yield new knowledge. Organizations may also choose to acquire knowledge from an outside source if it's cheaper than developing it internally – for example purchasing a list of potential customers.

Development

Knowledge development supports the acquisition of knowledge by generating new skills and ideas within the organization. It involves using the creativity of employees to produce new capabilities, improved processes, and innovative ideas.

Retention

Knowledge retention is the organization, storage, and maintenance of knowledge. Knowledge retention depends on the efficient use of electronic media.

Retention is particularly important when there's a high turnover of staff. If an organization's knowledge-retention mechanisms are poor, valuable expertise may be lost.

Distribution

Knowledge distribution involves making knowledge available to employees. It must be readily accessible, and easy to navigate when employees need it. Available, accurate, and high-quality knowledge is an asset to an organization.

In addition to training and knowledge management, technology is an important element that supports organizational learning. Organizations invest money, time, and resources in software tools to support the development of their knowledge libraries and sharing platforms. For instance, knowledge mapping – which involves mapping knowledge flows throughout an organization – uses surveys and auditing to track knowledge gains and losses. Flowcharting and concept map software programs are examples of programs that store, organize, and help develop knowledge.

Consider a senior management team using technology to help plan next year's budget. The team members can access internal storage data to provide them with sales figures and trends for previous years. They can also use the Internet to access knowledge on current industry and economic trends.

The management team can then use software tools to analyze, forecast, and understand present and future trends. In these ways, the management team is using technology to develop new insights and knowledge.

Technology is usually considered an integral part of an organization's strategy for survival and growth. However, an organization that simply uses technology is not automatically an effective learning organization.

In fact, investing in technology isn't the answer to increasing an organization's capacity for learning. It's simply a tool to facilitate and enhance learning. Although technology can help learners gather and share knowledge, it's of little help for organizations with poor knowledge management practices and defensive attitudes to change.

For leaders to develop a learning organization, they should first study how people learn in their workplace, and then use technology to support a learning culture.

The concept of learning is greater than the sum of its parts. Effective knowledge management systems, the latest technologies, and targeted training programs aren't sufficient on their own to maximize organizational learning. Leaders need to go beyond providing employees with enough information, training, and technology to allow them to do their jobs.

Organizations need to support a culture where employees are committed to self-development and continual self-improvement. In order to achieve this, organizational leaders need to nurture a culture of learning. This is the essential ingredient in successful organizational learning.

A learning culture exists where employees across the organization demonstrate positive learning attitudes, values, and practices. In addition, leaders support and prioritize continuous development for the organization and every employee.

Question

Which statements correctly reflect the relationship between training, knowledge management, technology, and organizational learning?

Options:

1. Training, knowledge management, and technology are tools that support organizational learning

2. An online knowledge library supports organizational learning if it's transparent and accessible

Developing a Culture of Learning

3. Knowledge management and technology make up the foundation of a learning culture
4. Effective knowledge management is the cornerstone of organizational learning

Answer:

Option 1: This option is correct. Effective training, efficient knowledge management practices, and supportive technology are all tools that facilitate organizational learning.

Option 2: This option is correct. Knowledge management supports organizational learning when it's transparent and accessible to employees as appropriate.

Option 3: This option is incorrect. Training, knowledge management, and technology are tools that work with a positive learning culture to support organizational learning.

Option 4: This option is incorrect. Effective knowledge management, technology, and training all support organizational learning, but they are not sufficient on their own. The essential ingredient is a pro-learning culture.

Elements of a learning culture

Training, technology, and knowledge management are important components that support organizational learning. Yet although they strengthen learning within an organization, they're not enough on their own. The true foundation for driving learning in an organization is a learning culture.

In a pro-learning culture, all employees accept a positive set of attitudes, values, and practices that support continuous learning. An organization's everyday practices will be dynamic, open, and inquisitive. Such a culture isn't limited to large multinational organizations – it can be developed in all sizes and types of organizations.

A learning culture has five key elements. The first is holistic thinking where employees understand how the parts of the organization interact and operate together. The second element is integrated and varied learning opportunities, designed to achieve a common goal. The third element is a capacity for continuous change and improvement. The fourth element is a focus on collaboration – learning and solving problems with others. Finally, the fifth element is personal commitment from all employees.

See each element to learn more.

Holistic thinking

Holistic thinking – or systems thinking – is the ability to see the "big picture" within an organization. Where holistic thinking exists, each and every employee understands how their work contributes to the overall strategy, and how changes in one area affect the whole organization.

Integrated learning opportunities

Integrated learning opportunities means learning through a variety of mechanisms. Learners may attend formal training, then reinforce and sustain what they learned through job shadowing, discussion, or on-the-job practice.

Integration also means making learning part of the job so that employees continually encounter opportunities to grow and develop as they carry out their responsibilities.

Capacity for change and improvement

A learning culture thrives when an organization has a capacity for change and improvement. In such cases, employees have an openness and willingness to accept change. They embrace change through continuous learning and discovery.

Focus on collaboration

A collaborative approach to learning – as opposed to an individualistic approach – focuses on learning as a group. A positive learning culture has collective thinking skills where a group has the capacity to develop a shared intellect. People learn from and with each other, and the combined intelligence of the group is greater than the sum of its individual members.

Personal commitment

Employees in a learning culture are motivated and committed to taking charge of their own learning. In a learning culture, individuals are proactive, and learning is largely self-directed.

Holistic thinking and integration

The first element of a learning culture is holistic thinking. A holistic perspective enables employees to understand interrelationships in the organization, and learn from them. When a problem exists, employees focus on identifying underlying causes, rather than treating symptoms in the short term. In a positive learning culture, employees understand the strategic importance of their actions. They consider the impact of their actions on other areas of the organization – in the present and in the future.

In order for a group of people to have a holistic approach to thinking, there must be a common organizational vision. A good vision motivates all members of an organization, giving them focus, regardless of their place in the organization.

For example, a payments administrator in a bank understands how his actions impact the organization. He knows that providing reliable, error-free service is part of the company's vision, and if he makes a mistake on a client account, it impacts the organization's reputation.

He also has an understanding of how his actions impact his colleagues in other departments. If he's late completing his work, he knows this affects his colleagues' ability to meet a deadline.

The second element of a learning culture is integrated learning opportunities. While formal training is one way to provide learning, it's not always the most effective. For learning to become permanent, it needs to be reinforced, applied, and sustained. This can be achieved by making diverse learning opportunities an integral part of everyday work practices.

It's important to provide employees with continuous reinforcing opportunities so they can practice what they have learned. This is most effective when employees are on the job and can apply what they've learned to their everyday tasks. Opportunities should be flexible, diverse, and targeted to learners' needs.

For example, Megan has just been trained on the company's internal web conferencing and remote support system. She's now observing her colleague Peter use the system to help a client navigate the company's online catalog. Peter then shows Megan how to navigate the system. Later, Megan can contact Peter via instant messaging on the company's intranet site to discuss any challenges that arise. Peter will also make himself available for ongoing support.

To help employees manage their diverse learning opportunities, organizations must provide good knowledge management and access to knowledge

Developing a Culture of Learning

resources. Employees should be able to easily access the information and resources they require for learning.

For example, Yvonne has moved to the derivatives processing team. She's not entirely comfortable with the mechanics of derivatives, so she accesses the organization's online library to learn how they work.

The library has recently been updated with the latest industry knowledge, so she's confident that she's learning best practices that will serve her in the future.

Question

Which statements are examples of elements of a learning culture?

Options:

1. An employee prioritizes other colleagues' tasks over his own
2. An employee has access to the information and resources she needs to learn about new products
3. An employee has frequent opportunities to learn and practice, allowing him to cement his learning
4. A manager uses a coach to help reinforce the delegation skills she learned in training
5. A manager ensures that each team member has equal training hours

Answer:

Option 1: This option is incorrect. Understanding how your work connects with the work of others reflects holistic thinking, but it doesn't require that you prioritize other colleagues' tasks over your own. It's important that you also consider the contribution of your own work to the organization.

Option 2: This option is correct. Good knowledge management and access to knowledge resources is an important part of providing integrated learning opportunities in a learning culture.

Option 3: This option is correct. Continuous, integrated opportunities to learn are evident in a positive learning culture.

Option 4: This option is correct. A manager seeking to reinforce classroom-based learning is an example of an integrated learning culture.

Option 5: This option is incorrect. Although managers must provide all employees with learning opportunities, ensuring an equal number of training hours does not represent an element of a learning culture.

Capacity for change and collaboration

The third element of a learning culture is an organization's capacity for change and improvement. Organizations that thrive in the long run are never satisfied with the status quo. They crave learning and improvement. Members of a positive learning culture continually challenge current processes and procedures to ensure accuracy and relevancy. They also challenge assumptions and perceptions about the internal and external environment.

An organization with a positive learning culture will challenge employees' "mental models." A mental model is a person's internal image of the environment.

Mental models shape decisions and behavior. They're based on deep-rooted assumptions, generalizations, or impressions that influence an individual's understanding of the world. Consequently, they influence that person's behavior and interactions with others.

When people are unaware of their mental models, they may not realize the effect they have on their colleagues. This may lead to missed opportunities to improve the way they work.

An organization that promotes learning must therefore confront mental models in employees. It should also promote self-awareness and self-improvement. Leaders can do this by probing and examining people's views – including their own – in open and honest forums, such as team meetings.

When employees are aware of their own assumptions and generalizations, they'll be less resistant and more open to change and improvement in the organization.

Of course, as a manager or leader, you shouldn't attempt to control employees' views. Employees should be encouraged to challenge superiors. They should feel free to scrutinize the organization and give constructive feedback through appropriate channels.

Consider Edward. He's a team leader in a bank. He realizes that his team – while dedicated and hard-working – is too focused on systems and processes. It's been months since the team took time to sit back and think strategically, so Edward calls a meeting to discuss his concerns.

Through the team members' feedback he realizes that they assumed their performance would be judged solely on meeting hard targets. Some team members felt that Edward undervalued interpersonal skills when considering the standard of their performance. Edward then decides to challenge the team's perception that he only focused on tangible outputs.

Developing a Culture of Learning

Through open dialog, the team members realize their assumption was based on hearsay. Edward then highlights his desire for more innovative ideas for process improvement. The team's willingness to challenge perceptions required reflection, analysis, critical thinking, and the courage to change.

The fourth element of a learning culture is a focus on collaboration. Collaboration is the social – or team – component of learning. It's important because positive relationships can enhance learning, while isolation or negative relationships can stifle learning. Adults learn best from each other by jointly reflecting on problems, putting information in context, questioning assumptions, and sharing feedback. Face-to-face interaction generates creative tension that motivates people to produce new ideas.

Successful team learning is based on synchronized action and respect for the opinions of others. Good knowledge management should ensure the free sharing of information, and networks should allow the development of knowledge and expertise.

A learning culture also has a climate of openness and trust to ensure meaningful dialog. Individuals are encouraged to freely and creatively explore issues together. Of course, meaningful dialog can't exist without everyone really listening to each other.

Consider Isabelle. She learns best when she can have robust discussions with her team. Isabelle finds that she has better ideas when she brainstorms with her colleagues, listens carefully, and considers their views.

Personal commitment

The fifth element of a learning culture is personal commitment from all employees. Organizations with a positive learning culture create an environment that encourages personal development within the scope of organizational goals. Employees are encouraged to take charge of their learning in a self-directed manner.

Relying on personal commitment from employees requires organizational leaders to work with the unique motivations of each employee. They need to acknowledge that their employees have individual styles, personal preferences, and motivators when it comes to learning. Tapping into these motivations and preferences can enable leaders to maximize each individual's potential.

Consider Ryan, a team leader. He achieves personal commitment from his team by making learning a rewarding experience. He listens to the needs of all his team members and accommodates their work styles and preferences as best he can. As a result, his team members feel motivated and have an incentive to develop their own potential.

For example, Ryan knows Brenda likes to learn with others. She loves lively in-person brainstorming sessions. Leanne on the other hand likes contributing her ideas and gleaning others' ideas on a message board. Ryan accommodates the preferences of both Brenda and Leanne whenever possible.

Such an environment, where employees are motivated, will encourage individuals to set personal goals for growth and development. If correctly managed, these will align with the organization's goals.

Question

Which statements are examples of elements of a learning culture?

Options:

1. Ian is determined to achieve a good work-life balance
2. Brian has continuous and reinforcing opportunities to practice the skills he learned on a recent course
3. Scott's delighted to be accepted to a management development program to improve his management skills
4. Mike's team uses collective thinking skills to solve a client issue
5. Anna relies on her manager to assign her learning objectives
6. Sandra is committed to taking charge and planning her own learning schedule

Answer:

Option 1: This option is incorrect. Ian looking after his own work-life balance doesn't reflect a learning culture. By only considering his own work-life balance, Ian fails to foster a learning culture.

Option 2: This option is correct. For Brian, continuous learning reinforced through integrated learning opportunities is an example of working in a learning culture.

Option 3: This option is correct. A learning culture thrives when there's a capacity for change and improvement. Scott is embracing change through continuous learning.

Option 4: This option is correct. When a team uses a collaborative approach to solving problems, a positive learning culture is fostered. By freely and creatively exploring solutions together, Mike's team can work toward solving the client's problem.

Option 5: This option is incorrect. In a learning culture, individuals such as Anna wouldn't depend on managers to direct their learning. They would show personal commitment through proactive and self-directed learning.

Option 6: This option is correct. In a learning culture, individuals such as Sandra show personal commitment. Learning tends to be proactive and self-directed.

Holistic thinking

Does your organization have a strong culture of learning? This may seem like a difficult question because an organization's culture is complex. It evolves through an accumulation of shared history, values, rules, and relationships.

A pro-learning culture provides a framework you can use to assess your own organization's culture and identify areas for improvement. There are five elements of a pro-learning culture:

- holistic thinking,
- integrated learning opportunities,
- a capacity for continuous change and improvement,
- a focus on collaboration, and
- personal commitment from all employees.

For each of the five elements there are key indicators of a pro-learning culture and an anti-learning culture. You can watch out for these indicators to help you evaluate the strength of your organization's learning culture.

The first element of a learning culture is holistic thinking. When people in an organization think holistically, they understand and consider the implications of their actions on the organization. Employees understand, for example, how their daily activities affect customer satisfaction and contribute to helping the organization achieve its strategic goals.

Furthermore, people at all levels of the organization – from senior management to entry-level employees – focus on a common vision and strategic direction.

An organization must include learning in its vision. To achieve this, managers should promote and share their vision for a positive learning culture.

One way managers can demonstrate their support for learning is to embrace learning opportunities themselves.

Managers should also coordinate their efforts across departments to achieve the organization's common learning goals.

You may have noted that when employees and managers don't think holistically, they think only of their own needs and desires without considering the implications of their actions. They also focus on individual, or personal, goals. In an anti-learning culture, management practices don't truly support a common vision of learning. Managers may discuss the importance of learning but fail to demonstrate support for it through their actions. They tend to work in isolation, focusing on departmental needs and self-promotion.

Question

Developing a Culture of Learning

Anna is a management consultant asked to assess the learning culture of a large-scale printing company. She interviews managers and employees to determine their regular practices and attitudes.

Which findings should Anna consider as evidence of holistic thinking about learning?

Options:

1. The management team meets monthly to organize six-week rotations of inter-departmental work placements
2. Employees are talking about how they're all working to make the company the top-rated customer service organization in the field
3. Department managers compete with each other for scarce resources
4. Managers approved ten times more learning opportunities for junior employees than they did for senior employees this year

Answer:

Option 1: This option is correct. Providing employees with learning opportunities in other departments is an example of holistic thinking.

Option 2: This option is correct. Employees working toward, and playing a part in, a common vision is an example of holistic thinking.

Option 3: This option is incorrect. Managers shouldn't be competing for scarce resources; they should be collaborating to find a solution that works for everyone.

Option 4: This option is incorrect. Holistically thinking leaders don't focus solely on junior staff. Leaders must ensure all employees devote time to learning.

Integrated learning

The second element of a learning culture is integrated learning opportunities. When there's an integrated approach, people at all levels of the organization participate in multimodal learning. It's important to use a variety of learning modes to accommodate the different learning needs of individuals. It also provides learners with reinforcement of new knowledge or skills. Multimodal learning could include, for example, a classroom-based management course supported by e-learning, on-the-job training, and one-on-one coaching.

On-the-job training is a good example of employees having the opportunity to regularly practice the skills they acquire through training or coaching. Such opportunities to practice – integrated into regular responsibilities and operations – put the new knowledge, skill, or behavior into context for the learner. Learning through real-life scenarios is more powerful than theory.

Developing a Culture of Learning

Good knowledge management supports integrated learning. Employees must have immediate access to up-to-date information to use on the job – for example procedures, process documents, or industry information.

Strong succession planning is another positive sign of integrated learning. Succession planning involves structuring employees' learning programs to prepare them for new roles and responsibilities beyond those they currently hold. It's an ongoing process that allows employees to continually stretch, develop, and improve their competencies.

Organizations with an integrated approach to learning also encourage employees to learn from a variety of external sources, looking to customers, suppliers, community groups, and others for learning experiences and feedback. Examples of opportunities to do so include conferences, industry events, and focus groups.

Consider Emma, who has recently joined a new company. Emma isn't settling into her job. So far she's received five days of classroom training, and has been shown to her desk to begin processing new client applications.

In training, Emma received a demonstration on how to process applications. She also has notes detailing what information to include, but this is her first time accessing the live system.

Emma reviews her training notes, and realizes some information is out of date. She accesses the company intranet, but finds the same information. She tries to ask a colleague for assistance, but he tells her to ask her manager.

Question

Do you think Emma received an integrated learning experience?

Options:

1. Yes
2. No

Answer:

In fact, Emma's learning would be considered one-dimensional. This is because it was a one-time classroom event and it wasn't supported by practice or on-the-job training.

Emma's organization shows signs of an anti-learning culture. Her one-dimensional, single classroom event isn't a good example of integrated learning. The organization is also poor at knowledge management, having out-of-date procedures on the intranet. What's more, Emma didn't receive any support from her colleague.

Question

Remember Anna, who's evaluating the learning culture of a printing company? She's now assessing the level of integrated learning.

Which findings should Anna consider as evidence that learning is integrated in that organization?

Options:

1. Employees have "learning hours" for either e-learning, exploring the knowledge bank, or observing colleagues.

2. The organization holds an annual conference with vendors and suppliers so employees can network.

3. New employees are allocated a "team buddy" for training and guidance in their first six months.

4. To learn management skills, new managers are given three days of classroom training.

5. The CEO reviews talent as required. The most capable employees are identified for promotion to open positions.

Answer:

Option 1: This option is correct. Allocating time for employees to take part in a diverse range of learning opportunities is an example of integrated learning.

Option 2: This option is correct. A conference is an example of providing employees with opportunities to learn industry knowledge from those outside the organization.

Option 3: This option is correct. On-the-job training is an important part of an integrated learning culture. It gives employees the confidence to practice and ask questions from colleagues.

Option 4: This option is incorrect. A few days of classroom training for new managers isn't considered sufficient in a pro-learning culture. Learning should be integrated with the job, comprehensive, and multimodal.

Option 5: This option is incorrect. In strong learning cultures, leaders support employee development through succession planning. They regularly identify promising employees to learn new roles and responsibilities while they're on the job.

Capacity for change and improvement
The third element of a learning culture is an organization's capacity for change and improvement. This capacity is evident in organizations where new recruits are hired and existing employees are evaluated based on their ability to learn and adapt – not just on their technical skills. Another key indicator of a pro-
learning organization is innovation. Adaptability and innovation should be common threads throughout all levels of the organization.

When assessing an organization's ability to change and continuously improve, it's important to consider whether employees at all levels are willing to explore their underlying assumptions and perceptions. This will be evident in their interactions with each other. Does critical inquiry exist in team discussions and decision making? Do people ask probing questions before drawing conclusions? Employees must be able to acknowledge assumptions,

Developing a Culture of Learning

avoid jumping to conclusions, and identify gaps between reality and perception.

In an organization where continuous change is promoted, employees will take time to reflect on current and future realities, considering multiple perspectives before acting.

For example, a group of employees consider the pros and cons of switching to the latest computer operating system. The employees discuss how the switch might draw in new customers. However, they realize that they might frustrate current customers whose systems aren't compatible.

Managers and leaders should view mistakes as learning opportunities, and tolerate and encourage experimentation. Continuous improvement is achieved through learning from experience.

Remember Emma? As a fresh pair of eyes on the client application process, she makes a suggestion for improvement to her manager. Her manager replies that the application process has always been done that way, and that Emma should just focus on learning her job.

Emma's manager demonstrates static thinking which will stifle, rather than nurture, a learning culture.

Focus on collaboration

The fourth element of a learning culture is a focus on collaboration. Indicators of a focus on collaboration include information sharing, good communication skills, group learning and decision making, and rewards for collaborative practices.

See each indicator to learn more.

Information sharing

In a pro-learning culture, employees and managers share information. For example, guidelines, processes, and procedures are freely available through shared resources – such as a shared drive or intranet site. People are proactive about sharing the lessons they've learned from experience.

Communication skills

Collaboration is much easier when employees have good communication skills. For example, when interacting with others, employees should have good

Developing a Culture of Learning

listening skills, show respect, and consider the opinions of others.

Group learning and decision making

All employees – managers and nonmanagers – must collaborate to learn and solve problems. As such, group learning and decision making should be standard practice.

Rewards for collaborative practices

Collaborative efforts should be rewarded. For example, employees who help new hires could receive formal recognition.

Question

Say you're a management consultant tasked with assessing an organization's learning culture. You've discovered that the sales manager, Peter, actively seeks out industry knowledge for his private database, which he occasionally shares with senior management.

Does the management team promote a positive learning culture by praising Peter publicly for his findings?

Options:

1. Yes
2. No

Answer:

n fact, there's evidence of an anti-learning culture. Peter hoards information and learns on his own. He shouldn't be rewarded for this failure to collaborate.

Personal commitment

The fifth element of a learning culture is personal commitment from all employees. Personal commitment is important to organizations as it drives employees to take charge of their own learning.

Question

Consider an organization where employees feel like "just a number" and take a passive approach to their development. Employees lack motivation to learn as they consider it to be a waste of time.

How has the organization failed to support the personal commitment of employees?

Options:

1. When employees feel unnoticed, they're more likely to take a passive approach to learning

2. The organization hasn't given employees enough credit for collaborative work

3. It's up to the employees, not the organization, to motivate themselves

Developing a Culture of Learning

Answer:

The organization should motivate employees. This can be achieved through treating everyone as an individual, and accommodating their different preferences and styles.

In a pro-learning culture, managers realize that energy comes from learning and growing, and they provide tailored opportunities and support to employees to match their unique needs. Employees are then more likely to take an active role in self-development, setting their own improvement goals, and directing their own learning. Personal commitment is evident when employees seek and take advantage of learning opportunities, and when they're recognized and rewarded for learning.

Now that you're familiar with the indicators of a pro-learning culture, consider Russel. He's a client services manager for a pension administration company. He's having a meeting with two of his team leaders, Liz and Eric. Follow along as Russel announces the introduction of a new client management system to their department.

Russel: OK, folks...I have an announcement. We're introducing a new client management system.

Liz: Hold on...what's wrong with the one we have? Liz is alarmed.

Russel: Oh, it's fine. But the new system has an interface that enables clients to manage their accounts online.

Liz: A new interface? There's going to be an uproar. You know how everyone reacted when management changed the payment processing functions.

Liz is exasperated.

Eric: Well I like it. I was at a conference last month, and they said there'd be a demand for this kind of service within three years.
Eric is enthusiastic.
Liz: So who's going to tell the teams? And, who's going to deal with the fallout? Not me anyway...
Liz is resentful.
Russel: I think we should all tell our own teams. So...you guys on board? Russel is persuasive.
Eric: I'm in! I'd like to get involved early. Maybe I could get on the project management team?
Eric is eager.
Russel: You bet...it'd be great to have an expert on the current system to keep things consistent.
Eric: And...maybe run some training too?
Eric is enthusiastic.
Liz: It's yours! None of the other team leaders will do it anyway!
Liz is dismissive.
Russel: But I can count on your help in some other way, right Liz?
Russel is encouraging.
Liz: Sure. So long as it goes on my record and you remember it when promotion time comes.
Liz is aggressive.
Russel: Let's talk about it later. We'll work on some new objectives for you.
Russel is diplomatic.

There are elements of Russel's situation that indicate a pro-learning culture. First, the senior management team demonstrates a commitment to change and improvement by adapting its client offerings in line with market demands.

Both Russel and Eric demonstrated adaptability by embracing the new system.

Eric showed his willingness and commitment to self-development. He took on board new industry information at the recent conference, and envisioned the potential for the organization. He also actively sought out opportunities to learn new skills from the project.

However, Liz's comments suggest that this is not a pro-learning culture. She demonstrated a static approach to thinking by suggesting the new system was unnecessary. Unlike Eric, Liz didn't consider the bigger picture.

Liz also indicated that many of the team leaders think like her. She also suggested that employees are resentful of change, and have reacted poorly in the past. Furthermore, rather than consider helping other employees adapt to the change, she refused to volunteer to collaborate with, and support, others in training.

Finally, Liz demonstrated a lack of commitment to self-development, and focused on taking individual credit for any contribution she was prepared to make.

Assessing the learning culture
Case Study: Question 1 of 4
Scenario

You now have a chance to practice assessing a culture for its capacity for change and improvement, focus on collaboration, and personal commitment. Consider Hazel and Max, operational team leaders for a logistics company. Hazel's team has recently been responsible for a missed delivery, costing the company a substantial sum in compensation to the customer. Company policy states that all process changes must be presented to the senior management team as a formal proposal. Also, all change request documents should be stored on the management network drive for other managers to access. Follow along as Hazel discusses the issue with Max.

Hazel: Got a minute? Huge problem on my team last week.

Hazel is frustrated.

Max: Sure...what happened?

Developing a Culture of Learning

Max is curious.

Hazel: That new subcontractor? Total communication breakdown with my team! We had to pay major compensation.

Hazel is exasperated.

Max: Why am I not surprised?

Max is laughing.

Hazel: Really...you've had this problem?

Hazel is curious.

Max: Oh, yeah! Two weeks ago. Same deal, big compensation...

Max is certain.

Hazel: I wish I'd known...Can we compare notes? How'd you handle it?

Hazel is curious.

Max: Well, for starters, I developed a process improvement plan...Presented it at the senior management meeting.

Max is proud.

Hazel: Really? When did all this happen?

Hazel is surprised.

Max: Just last week. But the team really came through. Everyone worked overtime...not a word of complaint!

Max is proud.

Hazel: Good for them! Can I take a look at your proposal? Could help us too.

Hazel is eager.

Max: Absolutely...Might even make me look better, come promotion time.

Max is laughing.

Hazel: Right. So...can I grab your proposal from the management drive?

Hazel is abrupt.
Max: It's on my personal drive. I'll e-mail it to you.
Max is willing.
Hazel: Thanks, Max.
Hazel is grateful.
Question
Which element of the discussion between Hazel and Max indicates a capacity for change and improvement?
Options:
1. Max says that he has implemented a process improvement plan
2. Hazel asks Max how he handled a similar issue to hers
3. Max agrees to share his process improvement plan with Hazel
Answer:
Option 1: This is the correct option. Following an error that cost the company a large compensation payment, Max was quick to implement changes that would reduce errors and the financial cost to the organization.

Option 2: This option is incorrect. Hazel demonstrates a collaborative effort by seeking input from Max.

Option 3: This option is incorrect. Max shows a willingness to collaborate by helping Hazel.

Case Study: Question 2 of 4
Which element of the discussion between Hazel and Max reflects collaborative learning?
Options:
1. Hazel praises Max's team for its success
2. Max tells Hazel that he developed a process improvement plan

3. Hazel asks Max how he handled a similar problem to hers

Answer:

Option 1: This option is incorrect. Hazel congratulating Max's team for its success is not a demonstration of learning through collaboration.

Option 2: This option is incorrect. Max revealing the existence of a new process isn't an indication of collaborative learning.

Option 3: This is the correct option. Seeking information about Max's experience represents an attempt by Hazel to learn collaboratively.

Case Study: Question 3 of 4

Which elements of the discussion between Hazel and Max indicate personal commitment to learning?

Options:

1. Hazel wants to improve how her team works by using Max's process improvement plan
2. Max keeps the process improvement plan on his personal drive
3. Max believes that sharing the process improvement plan will help him get promoted
4. Max creates a process improvement plan

Answer:

Option 1: This is a correct option. Hazel demonstrates a commitment to self-directed learning with her desire to apply a helpful new approach.

Option 2: This option is incorrect. By keeping important information on his personal drive, Max isn't following procedures. It should be on the management drive.

Option 3: This option is incorrect. Max's comment doesn't demonstrate that he's committed to learning, but that he seeks credit for sharing.

Option 4: This option is correct. Max took the initiative to improve his team's productivity and success through learning.

Case Study: Question 4 of 4

Based on the dialog between Max and Hazel, what would you judge to be the strongest element of this organization's learning culture?

Options:

1. Personal commitment and a capacity for change and improvement
2. Collaboration and a capacity for change and improvement
3. Collaboration and personal commitment

Answer:

Option 1: This is the correct option. Both Max and Hazel demonstrated strong elements of personal commitment and a capacity to improve processes on their teams.

Option 2: This option is incorrect. Both Max and Hazel showed a capacity to make process changes, but Max lacked a willingness to collaborate.

Option 3: This option is incorrect. Both Max and Hazel revealed a personal commitment to learning and improvement, but Max should be more willing to collaborate.

CHAPTER TWO
Establishing the Conditions for a Learning Culture

The case for a learning culture

In the modern business world with its conflicting demands, people often miss the chance to learn. Learning is a long-term change in knowledge, skills, understanding, or conduct. Learning may also involve discarding knowledge that's no longer valid.

Organizations that want to adapt quickly to changing business environments need to promote organizational learning and foster a learning culture. Organizational learning is improved employee competence gained through continuous improvement. A learning culture reflects beliefs and practices that encourage continuous development. Employees working in a learning culture embrace continuous self-development.

In any workplace, there's a feedback loop between culture and feelings.

It works like this: people's feelings determine their behavior, and people's behaviors influence their environment. In turn, behaviors and environment – which make up the workplace culture – influence feelings. The cycle continues when feelings go on to affect behaviors.

It's important to establish a positive atmosphere surrounding culture and feelings. If people feel positively about learning, and they see learning behaviors reinforced in the workplace, they will continue to seek out learning opportunities.

A strong learning culture creates a balance between feelings of doubt and security, which enhances motivation for and receptivity to learning.

See each way that culture affects learning to learn more about it.

Balance of doubt and security

When people are doubtful, they need to inquire into a situation to resolve the discomfort of not knowing. Doubt provides the impetus to solve a puzzle or resolve a contradiction, for example. Doubt is the tension needed to examine issues more closely, and to be open to learning new things. However, too much doubt can be threatening.

People also need to feel secure to challenge ideas, share their thoughts, and acknowledge error. Strong learning cultures strike a balance between creative tension and security to explore.

Motivation for learning

Workplace learning is often voluntary and self-directed. In a strong learning culture, people are motivated to learn.

Receptivity to learning

In a strong learning culture, people sense and take advantage of learning opportunities they encounter. They are receptive to learning that comes in a variety of forms, including formal, planned learning, learning from mistakes, and even learning unintentionally.

Establishing the right balance of doubt and security, and encouraging positive feelings about change and improvement, leads to pro-learning behaviors that set the tone in the workplace environment.

Once the environment, in turn, exerts a positive impact on feelings, you'll begin to benefit from the reciprocal nature of feelings, behavior, and environment.

At this point, you may detect a culture of learning taking root in your organization.

Question

Which statements describe the relationship between organizational culture and learning?

Options:

1. Individuals are ready to take advantage of various types of learning opportunities

2. People have the urge to develop and learn

3. The culture counteracts the stress of an inquiring nature with the freedom to explore safely

4. People's feelings and behaviors set a tone in the workplace, which goes on to influence feelings and behaviors

5. A culture of doubt is most conducive to organizational learning

6. Managers' behaviors determine whether or not an organizational culture supports learning

Answer:

Option 1: This option is correct. A culture that encourages people to take advantage of learning opportunities affects receptivity to learning.

Option 2: This option is correct. Workplace learning is usually voluntary and self-directed. In such an environment people want to grow, improve, and learn.

Option 3: This option is correct. A culture that balances doubt and security encourages learning.

Option 4: This option is correct. Encouraging positive feelings capitalizes on the reciprocal relationship by encouraging pro-learning feelings and behaviors. In this culture, people will look for learning opportunities.

Option 5: This option is incorrect. You need a balance of doubt and security. This enhances motivation for learning and receptivity to learning.

Option 6: This option is incorrect. Managers' behaviors alone don't determine whether or not the organizational culture supports learning. The feelings and behaviors of all employees influence organizational culture.

Key conditions for a learning culture

A learning culture doesn't develop by accident. Organizations can encourage learning by having the right conditions in place.

You may have noted that a freedom to explore is a key condition. Equally important is a habit of reflection that leads people to learn from the past and present. You may have noted that learning is supported by egalitarian relationships and collaborative practices – both key conditions that underlie a learning culture. But perhaps the most important condition is an organization-wide motivation for learning and growth.

The first condition to establish a strong learning culture is the freedom to explore.

Under this condition, people are free to explore others' thoughts, opinions, and actions. They can also question the reasoning behind these thoughts or opinions.

This open atmosphere increases the chances of getting information vital to learning. It encourages full, honest disclosure.

To establish the freedom to explore in his team, a manager of a support group reserves 30 minutes at each team meeting to allow people to bring up new ideas to improve performance.

During this segment all ideas are discussed constructively – everyone is encouraged to discuss the ideas of others and to ask questions.

The manager doesn't criticize any mistakes that are uncovered, rather he encourages people to learn how to avoid repeating the same mistakes.

The second condition to establish a strong learning culture is a habit of reflection. Employees with a habit of reflection are inquiring, objective, and analytical.

See each aspect of a habit of reflection to learn more about it.

Inquiring

People who have an inquiring nature are persistent. They get to the core of a situation by asking open questions to identify gaps and inconsistencies.

Objective

Objectivity is the ability to overcome personal feelings about a subject and perceive it as it is. This includes resisting the human temptation of claiming credit for success and excusing failure.

Analytical

Being analytical means that people reflect on their experiences. The intent is to build a complete picture of any situation.

Think about this situation. The IT manager at an online music vendor encourages his team to gather information from the customer service team to analyze complaints regarding the payment process.

The manager tells the team members they're expected to find the root cause of these issues. They're also asked to develop plans to make the payment process more user-friendly.

Members of the IT team examine each customer requirement in detail. They find that some requirements are already features in the system – meaning they should be better communicated to customers. User-friendly enhancements are developed that make the online check-out process 20% quicker for customers.

Having egalitarian relationships is the third condition necessary to establish a learning culture. Egalitarianism promotes power sharing, participation, and responsibility at all levels of the organization.

Egalitarian relationships promote equal responsibility for, and participation in, learning. They open up communication channels to innovation and learning.

Consider the egalitarian culture at an IT support helpdesk. Everyone on the helpdesk has a say in developing the department's learning strategies. So managers, team leaders, and employees are equally accountable for the success or failure of the learning strategies.

Question

Which conditions are necessary for establishing a learning culture?

Options:

1. Freedom to explore

2. Egalitarian relationships
3. Clear hierarchies
4. Employee behavior policies
5. Habit of reflection

Answer:

Option 1: This option is correct. To develop a learning culture, people should be free to experiment, and to explore thoughts and actions.

Option 2: This option is correct. Egalitarian relationships open up communication channels to innovation and learning.

Option 3: This option is incorrect. Rigid hierarchies don't help to establish a learning culture. Egalitarianism helps you to establish a learning culture.

Option 4: This option is incorrect. Employee policies don't help to establish a learning culture. The freedom to explore helps you to establish a learning culture.

Option 5: This option is correct. People with a habit of reflection are inquiring, objective, and analytical – all qualities that catalyze learning.

Encouraging collaborative practices is the fourth condition to establish a learning culture. Collaborative practices involve people working together to share what they know with others and to learn along with them. This brings about a feeling of belonging and participation and, in turn, fosters a learning culture.

Imagine this situation. A senior manager encourages his staff members to learn more about different aspects of the business. The staff members are told to ask for whatever information they want, without needing to justify the request.

When a new product development initiative is announced, Research Department staff members feel empowered to ask the Marketing Department about the latest research in market trends. Marketing staff members, in turn, ask about new product features from the Research Department.

After six months, the senior manager notes an improvement in employee knowledge about different business areas.

The fifth condition to establish a learning culture is motivation for learning and growth. Motivation is the natural urge to achieve a desired goal. Motivation to learn is enabled by a person's interest and enjoyment of learning. People who are motivated to learn do so quickly, comprehensively, and creatively. They are most strongly motivated to learn when they feel that responsibility and ownership for learning lies within their own hands.

Consider the situation of a junior administrator at an online travel company. The administrator enjoys learning and developing her capabilities.

Over time, she takes on the responsibility for planning the training she wants to attend. She always selects training that she enjoys and that will further her career prospects.

Within two years her efforts are rewarded with a promotion and a college qualification.

Question

What examples represent conditions that foster a strong learning culture?

Options:

1. Employees can question new product ideas

Developing a Culture of Learning

2. Employees are encouraged to analyze the entire assembly process

3. All quality assurance team members have a stake in the team's deliverables

4. A CEO says that 25% of the employee bonus depends on people's ability to work with others and share data

5. An employee readily takes advantage of the company's study leave policy to take a course 6. Information is obtained on a "need-to-know" basis

7. IT staff members are encouraged to focus on their routine tasks

Answer:

Option 1: This option is correct. Employees have the freedom to explore because they can question the reasoning behind new products. This open atmosphere increases the chances of obtaining vital information.

Option 2: This option is correct. A habit of reflection allows assembly workers to get a complete picture of the assembly process. Reflection enables people to analyze and learn from experiences.

Option 3: This option is correct. Egalitarian relationships allow all team members to have a stake in team deliverables. Egalitarianism promotes responsibility at all levels.

Option 4: This option is correct. Reserving part of the annual bonus for information sharing encourages collaborative practices. Collaboration promotes sharing and participation and so fosters a learning culture.

Option 5: This option is correct. Motivation is the natural urge to achieve a goal. Motivation to learn is enabled by a person's interest and enjoyment of learning.

Option 6: This option is incorrect. Restricting information isn't a condition for a learning culture. Freedom to explore is a condition for a learning culture to develop.

Option 7: This option is incorrect. Encouraging staff to focus on routine doesn't support a learning culture. On the other hand, collaborative practices and exploration are conditions for a strong learning culture.

Obstacles to a learning culture

Your organizational culture can encourage learning but it can also present obstacles that you, as a leader, need to overcome. These can stem from either human nature or the nature of organizations. Obstacles include intolerance of mistakes, common mental biases, hierarchical thinking, isolation, and inertia.

Intolerance of mistakes is a formidable obstacle to learning. In many organizations, people at all levels are fearful of making mistakes because they are punished for making them. When they do make mistakes, they tend to hide them, or explain them away.

Why is this an obstacle to learning? Intolerance of mistakes stifles experimentation and risk-taking. Intolerance of mistakes also prevents people from learning from mistakes – if people don't acknowledge and analyze their mistakes, they can't learn from them.

Imagine this situation at an airline. The Ticketing Department has used an out-of-date price file to price tickets. The department manager, fearing disciplinary action, covers up the error. Two months later, the Reservations Department repeats the mistake using the same price file. Fear has prevented the manager from learning from the mistake and sharing his experience with others – thus causing the same mistake to be repeated.

Mental bias is another obstacle to establishing a learning culture. Several common biases are naturally ingrained in our thinking. People use them to make sense of the world and process information. Brains don't store information in the orderly way a computer does. Instead, people unconsciously edit information and merge new and old information. In the process, they introduce bias. Common mental biases include hindsight bias, jumping to conclusions, taking credit for success and rationalizing failures, and feeling you know it all.

See each bias to learn more about it.

Hindsight bias

When outcomes seem inevitable after the fact, people are suffering from hindsight bias. Thinking that you "knew it all along" is an illusion that prevents learning from experience.

An example of hindsight bias might be if a company adds new features to a product, but the features fail to ignite customer interest. Six months later, a product director claims he always knew that customers wouldn't be interested in the new features.

As time passes, people become convinced that they could have predicted the eventual outcome. It's hard for people to imagine how they perceived the situation before they knew what the outcome would be. But until they can go back and understand what their earlier thinking was, they may not fully analyze and learn from the experience.

Jumping to conclusions

People jump to conclusions when they don't have time or can't make sense of information. This impedes learning because they don't arrive at the right conclusion and so don't learn from experience.

Imagine this example. A brand manager launches a new grocery item only to discover that, despite a national advertising campaign, the product's sales are low. He quickly concludes that this high-end dessert product would have been better suited to the food-service market instead of retail because people will pay a lot for desserts in restaurants but not in grocery stores. Because he jumped to this conclusion, he did not realize that their advertising campaign had failed to reach their target market due to the time of day the TV ads aired and the networks they aired on.

Taking credit for success and rationalizing failures

Taking credit for success and rationalizing failures causes some employees to overestimate their abilities and helps them avoid the pain of admitting mistakes. It's very tempting to explain away failures. However, employees can only learn from mistakes they acknowledge.

Suppose the cost estimations for a new product are off by 3%. The project manager blames this on "unforeseen circumstances." So the real reason – a lack of estimation competence – goes unlearned.

Feeling you know it all

Feeling you know it all arises from not analyzing and reflecting on experiences. When people think they know what they need to know, they aren't receptive to new information. This impedes learning because it prevents analysis and learning from experience.

Imagine this example. The sales VP thinks he knows all about market trends in his sales area. Because of this, he doesn't call a sales review meeting to get his subordinates' perspectives on the market. Consequently he misses an opportunity to learn new insights about the market.

The third obstacle to establishing a learning culture is hierarchical thinking. This thinking casts managers and leaders as the thinkers and lower-level employees as the doers who implement the leaders' ideas. This makes nonmanagers feel their ideas aren't valued. Or, they don't feel empowered to challenge leaders' ideas.

Hierarchies are an obstacle to learning because they may prevent people at all levels of seniority from being honest about what they know, what they don't know, and what they need to know. Innovation can also be stifled because it can't flourish unless employees are encouraged to think for themselves.

Say that a marketing VP comes up with a new concept for a mobile Internet product. The VP and other senior executives use their creativity to specify the product's features. However, other employees don't feel free to contribute their ideas to the specifications. The result is that good ideas are missed and nonmanagers, such as engineers, don't have opportunities to improve the product.

Isolation is the fourth obstacle to a learning culture. People are isolated when they work in organizational silos, and have limited interaction with people who have different perspectives. People also become isolated when information is handed out on a "need-to-know" basis.

For example, a salesperson may want to understand the features of a new product under development. If this information is tightly held in the Engineering Department, the salesperson can't learn more about the product and use the information in a customer presentation.

Isolation is an obstacle to learning because it prevents collaborative learning. Learning has a social aspect. To enable learning to flourish, leaders should foster relationships between people so that they can convey what they've learned and how they've learned it. It's difficult to do this in an isolating environment.

The fifth obstacle to a learning culture is inertia. Routines and conventions contribute to inertia. Employees may be comfortable with a current process and reluctant to improve it, even though there are efficiencies to be gained by changing the process. Coupled with an unwillingness to "think outside the box," inertia stifles the motivation to learn. Worse, it impairs efforts to overcome the other obstacles to learning.

Question

Match each obstacle to the description of how it impairs learning.

Options:

A. Intolerance of mistakes
B. Mental bias
C. Hierarchical thinking
D. Isolation
E. Inertia

Targets:

1. Blocks people from experimenting and taking chances

2. Leads to the wrong conclusion and so inhibits learning from experience

3. Stops people at all levels from being honest about what they need to know

4. Prevents people from learning in collaboration with others

5. Stifles the motivation to learn

Answer:

In many organizations, people are afraid to take risks because mistakes aren't tolerated.

Common biases such as hindsight bias and rationalization of failure impede learning because people don't arrive at the right conclusions and so don't learn from experience.

Hierarchical thinking may impede learning by preventing people at various levels of seniority from being honest about what they know, what they don't know, and what they need to know.

Workplace conventions that sustain isolation prevent people from optimizing their learning through collaboration and sharing.

Routines and conventions can contribute to inertia and impede growth and improvement.

The freedom to explore

There are five key conditions to establish a learning culture. These are the freedom to explore, a habit of reflection, egalitarian relationships, collaborative practices, and motivation for learning and growth. As a leader, you'll likely face a number of human and organizational obstacles that make it challenging to establish these conditions.

The first condition to establish a learning culture is the freedom to explore. Intolerance of mistakes, and the tendency to hide mistakes are the main obstacles you'll need to overcome in order to establish this condition. You can foster the freedom to explore by encouraging transparency, treating mistakes as learning experiences, and focusing on the issues rather than personal reactions.

The first action to overcome intolerance of mistakes is to encourage transparency. Where there's transparency, people can clearly and honestly reveal their actions, thoughts, and plans – and the reasoning behind these. One way to achieve this is to admit mistakes.

Where there's transparency, there's more likely to be full, honest disclosure, and you're more likely to get accurate information. It also lowers the chances of self-deception. In other words, it enables learning by giving people the information they need to question themselves and others.

For example, a marketing VP admits to her team that the focus group conducted for new product research was aimed at the wrong demographic. The product was a low-calorie snack aimed at women aged 24-50, but the focus group included men, children, and seniors. Because the VP urges her team members to question how she sets up focus groups, they'll be more likely to provide their ideas and input in the future.

The second action to overcome intolerance of mistakes is to treat them as learning experiences.

Tolerating mistakes is important because it gives people the freedom to experiment and then learn from the results. Of course, people must be willing to admit to mistakes if they're to learn from them.

Consider this example where a mistake is tolerated and measures are put in place to prevent its recurrence. A manager at a consulting company fails to adequately resource a customer project. When the mistake is detected, she admits it to her boss, who asks her what she would do differently in the future. The manager says she'll give more time to resource planning in all future projects.

Question

Which action would help you to foster the freedom to explore?

Developing a Culture of Learning

Options:

1. Create an environment where people can reveal their plans to deal with missed project deadlines

2. Create an environment where people are discreet about errors in resolving customer complaints

3. Create a document security system where people can keep information secret

Answer:

Option 1: This is the correct option. Revealing information increases transparency, which makes people less secretive and timid about revealing mistakes. This frees people to explore and take risks.

Option 2: This option is incorrect. If you want to foster the freedom to explore, freely discuss errors and treat them as learning experiences.

Option 3: This option is incorrect. Encouraging secrecy doesn't enable the freedom to explore. Instead, you should encourage transparency.

To create a learning culture, don't punish mistakes. Instead, address the failure to learn from mistakes. That is, only take action if your people don't recognize their mistakes or continue to repeat their mistakes. Think again about the manager at the consulting company. If she repeats her resourcing mistake and her next project falls behind schedule, her boss would be justified in taking disciplinary action – not because she made an error, but because she failed to learn from her previous one.

The third action to overcome intolerance of mistakes is to focus on the issues. This means making judgments based on facts rather than on politics or prejudice. It means asking about what happened rather than looking for who to blame when something goes wrong.

For example, a quality assurance director finds problems with a new quality process, which he traces back to inconsistencies in the process documentation.

Instead of finding someone to blame, the director focuses his efforts on trying to find out what should be corrected in the process documentation.

Question

Which statements are examples of actions that nurture the freedom to explore?

Options:

1. A sales manager reveals a pricing error that leads to a lost sale. The sales VP tells the manager to devote more time to pricing in all future bids.

2. When a software release causes customers to complain, the head of engineering wants to find out why the release process failed.

3. A manager tells the engineering VP that some features were left out of a product release. The VP responds by taking disciplinary action against the manager.

4. A finance director always tells an accountant to sign off on the monthly balance sheets without examining them.

Answer:

Option 1: This option is correct. Treating mistakes as learning experiences nurtures the freedom to explore and enables others to learn from mistakes.

Option 2: This option is correct. Focusing on the issues by asking what went wrong nurtures the freedom to explore by avoiding a blame culture.

Option 3: This option is incorrect. Punishing mistakes in a product release doesn't nurture a freedom to explore.

Treating mistakes as learning experiences encourages people to explore.

Option 4: This option is incorrect. Discouraging the examination of balance sheets lowers transparency. This impedes the freedom to explore and learn from mistakes.

A habit of reflection

The second condition necessary for a learning culture is a habit of reflection. Promoting a habit of reflection means encouraging a sense of curiosity and inquiry. Common mental biases may obstruct your efforts to establish this condition. But by cultivating a habit of reflection yourself, you encourage reflection in your colleagues and team members too.

As a leader, you can encourage curiosity and inquiry by showing a willingness to explore a situation in detail and investigating all relevant information. This involves asking open questions, gathering information, and spotting flaws and contradictions in strategies, plans, or arguments.

A manufacturer of marine GPS tracking devices used by research scientists to track whales finds that the units are failing occasionally. Support engineers examine the last recorded depth of each unit when it failed, but find no correlation between depth and failure. The engineers conclude that depth isn't the problem.

But a research manager questions this assumption. Looking closer at the data, she discovers that the greatest depth the animal reached within the last 24 hours clearly correlated with failure, with more failures at greater depths. The manager concludes that the pressure placed on tracking units at greater depths doesn't cause them to fail immediately, but does within 24 hours.

It's critical to check your information to separate fact from assumption. Make a habit of fact-checking before making decisions and insist that others do so too.

Encouraging reflection is important because it increases the likelihood of perceiving reality as it is. Reflection also enables learning from experience. This is especially the case when there's a gap between predictions and actual outcomes.

Question

Which actions enable a habit of reflection?

Options:

1. Promoting the need to know
2. Promoting curiosity
3. Encouraging transparency
4. Encouraging personal wellness practices

Answer:

Option 1: This option is correct. Asking open questions encourages people to gather information and find out more. You can encourage curiosity and inquiry by showing a willingness to explore situations.

Option 2: This option is correct. Encouraging a sense of curiosity pushes people to inquire, question, and learn. By cultivating a habit of reflection yourself, you encourage the habit in others.

Option 3: This option is incorrect. Encouraging transparency enables the freedom to explore. Encouraging curiosity and inquiry enables a habit of reflection.

Option 4: This option is incorrect. Encouraging personal wellness doesn't enable a habit of reflection. Promoting inquiry, curiosity, and scrutiny helps to overcome common mental biases and establish a habit of reflection.

One way of becoming more reflective is to make a habit of comparing predictions with outcomes after an event has occurred. This involves five steps.

First, define what success or failure means and record your predictions. After the event, once you know what the outcome is, compare your predictions to the outcomes.

Then ask what you could have done differently, and ask for feedback from others.

Consider this situation. Robert, a quality manager for a furniture manufacturer, engages in this process of comparing predictions to outcomes. He questions his team's ability to deliver a mandated 10% reduction in manufacturing defects in the next quarter.

See each step in order to learn more about it and get an example from Robert's situation.

1. Define success or failure

During this step, you specify what constitutes success or failure and determine the methods you'll use to measure results.

Robert defines success as a 10% reduction in manufacturing defects.

2. Record predictions

The second step is to record your predictions. This step prevents hindsight bias from creeping into interpretations of the outcome. It reveals what you were thinking before you knew what the result would be, and sets you up to learn from an unexpected outcome.

Two experienced quality engineers have left Robert's company. Also, his team is under pressure to deliver in other areas. So Robert predicts that process improvements will take 5 weeks to roll out, and by the end of this period, defects will be down 9%.

3. Compare predictions to outcomes

The third step is to compare your predictions to actual outcomes.

After six months, Robert compares his prediction to the outcome. The team only delivered a 3% drop in defects. Robert has failed to accurately predict the outcome.

4. Ask what you could have done differently

If the results don't match your predictions of success, the fourth step is to ask yourself what you could have done differently. If you were successful, identify the factors that were responsible for your success.

Robert believes that he should have coached weaker team members in improvement methods, and reassigned more experienced people to the project.

5. Ask for feedback from others

As a final step, ask for feedback from others. They're likely to give a detached appraisal and offer insights you hadn't considered.

Robert asks the sales VP to review his predictions and the outcome. The VP tells Robert that, in the future, he could argue for more resources to support his goal.

Robert's actions have helped him to perceive the reality of the resource issue on his team. His reflections on the outcome of his predictions and feedback from others have taught him how to deal with similar situations in the future.

You can use this process to optimize learning in training situations too. When trainers present case studies, it's best for them to withhold the case outcomes until learners have had a chance to make and record their predictions.

After the result is revealed, learners can compare their predictions with results.

Question

Which actions help to foster a habit of reflection?

Options:

1. An HR manager records predictions of how employees will perform in their jobs

2. A manager analyzes predictions of product quality against current quality metrics

3. A quality manager questions if a test process is effective in finding assembly defects

4. A sales VP verifies the assumption that a 15% sales increase is due to improved quality

5. An engineer records a list of successes and failures as they occur

6. A manager is more interested in analyzing failures than successes

Answer:

Option 1: This option is correct. Recording predictions enables the manager to compare forecasts with realities, which in turn reduces the effect of hindsight bias.

Option 2: This option is correct. Comparing predictions to outcomes enables you to learn from reflecting on the differences between them.

Option 3: This option is correct. Adopting an inquiring attitude to testing fosters reflection. Inquiring into a situation helps to build a more complete picture of it.

Option 4: This option is correct. Checking the facts behind a sales increase fosters a habit of reflection. Insist that everyone in the organization check their facts.

Option 5: This option is incorrect. Merely recording successes and failures isn't enough. Reflection happens when teams scrutinize outcomes and compare them with predictions.

Option 6: This option is incorrect. Reflecting on the factors that contribute to success is as valuable a learning experience as analyzing what went wrong with failures.

Egalitarian relationships

The third condition to establish a learning culture is egalitarian relationships. Egalitarianism helps to reinforce a sense of safety, fairness, and participation in the organization.

Hierarchical thinking is an obstacle you'll need to overcome in order to create egalitarian relationships.

To counter hierarchical thinking, you should promote egalitarian relationships by treating people equitably, regardless of rank. This helps generate trust and openness between people at all levels.

Imagine this situation. Assembly workers at a computer manufacturer find that it takes too much time to install motherboards. The assembly workers, senior engineers, and manufacturing VP all work together to come up with a solution. It involves changing the order of some installation steps and merging others.

In the process of discussing installation methods they open up communications and learn techniques and process improvements from each other. The VP learned about manufacturing procedures and the assemblers learned about motherboard technology.

The VP noted the valuable input from everyone involved and acknowledged their help in solving the problem.

Collaborative practices

The fourth condition required to support a learning culture is the establishment of collaborative practices. Collaboration is key to learning because it leads to knowledge generation and sharing. The creative tension that results from face-to-face interaction is a force that drives and enhances learning.

But in many workplaces, group work is seen as time intensive and unnecessary. Isolation develops where customs and organizational silos prevent people from working in partnerships and groups.

How do you overcome these isolating tendencies? You can provide opportunities to interact and learn and you can encourage people to seek feedback, information, and perspectives from a variety of sources inside and outside the organization.

Question

Match each action to the way it supports learning.

Options:

A. Promoting transparency
B. Tolerating mistakes
C. Facilitating reflection
D. Promoting egalitarianism
E. Promoting collaboration

Targets:

1. Increases the likelihood of obtaining valid information by encouraging complete disclosure

2. Makes it easier for people to experiment and learn from their experiments

3. Increases the likelihood of perceiving reality correctly

4. Opens up the channels of communication between various levels of the organization

5. Generates events where information and learning are shared

Answer:

Transparency encourages more open disclosure and communication of information.

Tolerance facilitates experimentation by making people feel free to take reasonable risks.

Facilitating reflection increases the accuracy of perceptions and enables learning from experiences and feedback.

Egalitarianism opens up communication and encourages information sharing and learning at all levels of seniority.

The creative tension and knowledge sharing between people when they collaborate enhances learning.

When people have opportunities to interact with others, they develop new perspectives. For example, an insurance company sends a team to gather best practices from each regional sales office. The team discovers new sales techniques from experts they respect in each regional office. Along the way, the team shares and refines these findings through lively best-practice discussions in each sales office. Existing knowledge is distributed and new knowledge is generated, leading to a permanent change in the organization's collective knowledge.

Interacting with others can lead to creative tension that motivates people to learn and change. Consider another situation where analysts from the Engineering, Support, and Marketing Departments in a company are told that a graphics application has failed because customers don't like the user interface. There's some doubt about this conclusion, so the analysts are asked to uncover the real problem.

The analysts work together to uncover the real problem. The engineering analyst challenges Marketing's belief that some requirements were omitted. In turn, the support analyst questions the engineer's belief that some features went untested. They're all motivated by the need to uncover the root of the problem and by their interaction with each other.

Jointly, the analysts write a report concluding that some crucial user requirements were omitted and others were tested insufficiently. The team used creative discussions to come to some valuable conclusions. In the process they learned about different aspects of the business in a collaborative environment.

Encouraging employees to seek feedback, information, and perspectives from various internal and external sources is important because most people aren't aware of the tremendous pool of knowledge that's available to them. Consequently, they use only a fraction of the knowledge available in their organization. Much of the information needed isn't documented – it's in people's heads.

Examples of sources of perspectives and feedback might include customers, vendors, and business partners.

Imagine that a production engineer in a manufacturing facility needs to understand the best way to set up a production process.

She seeks a well-rounded view of the process by first asking assembly line workers for their opinions on the best use of automation in the production process.

Then she finds out about the latest thinking in production quality standards by soliciting advice from an external consultant. She realizes that the more sources she seeks out, the more complete her assessment of the issue will be.

Question

Match the conditions that foster a learning culture to example strategies for establishing them. You may use each condition more than once.

Options:

A. Egalitarian relationships
B. Collaborative practices

Targets:

1. Encouraging employees at all organizational levels in the company to contribute product ideas

2. Asking employees from different departments to work together to fix a product defect

3. Making everyone responsible for a product's failure, regardless of seniority

4. Encouraging the Marketing Department to gather new product input from customers, suppliers, and internal sales people

5. Giving all employees a voice in the company's strategic direction

Answer:

Fostering egalitarian relationships involves making employees at all levels feel their input is valued, and encouraging them to contribute ideas.

Collaborative practices involve employees working together. These foster learning by creating opportunities for people to learn from each other.

Egalitarian relationships make everyone responsible for a success or failure.

Collaborative practices involve gathering information from internal and external sources. Much of the information needed could be inside people's heads.

Egalitarianism means that all employees have a voice in the company's strategic direction. It opens up communication channels so people can learn from each other.

The conditions for a learning culture

Taken together, the first four conditions covered in this topic will help set the stage for a healthy learning culture to thrive in your organization. But they are not enough on their own. Perhaps the most critical condition comes from employees themselves: the motivation to learn and grow.

Case Study: Question 1 of 3

Scenario

Joan is the HR director at a medical devices company. She wants to promote a culture of learning by establishing egalitarian relationships and collaborative practices, as she feels these areas are particularly weak in her company.

Answer the questions in the given order.

Question

Joan recognizes a number of weaknesses in her organization's culture.

Which obstacles will Joan have to overcome to establish egalitarian relationships and collaborative practices?

Options:

1. The perception that leaders are "thinkers" and employees are "doers"
2. Lack of shared responsibility or power when it comes to deciding product strategy
3. Rigid organizational divisions between departments
4. The tendency to cover up executives' mistakes
5. The tendency to jump to conclusions

Answer:

Option 1: This option is correct. The perception that leaders are "thinkers" and employees are "doers" is an obstacle to egalitarian relationships. Promoting equity counters hierarchical thinking.

Option 2: This option is correct. Hierarchical thinking is perpetuated when responsibility and power aren't shared.

Option 3: This option is correct. Rigid organizational structures prevent people from communicating across departments by isolating them.

Option 4: This option is incorrect. Covering up mistakes isn't an obstacle to egalitarian relationships or collaborative practices. It's a barrier to free exploration and experimentation.

Option 5: This option is incorrect. Jumping to conclusions isn't an obstacle to egalitarian relationships or collaborative practices. It's an obstacle to careful reflection and learning from the past.

Case Study: Question 2 of 3

What actions should Joan take to establish egalitarian relationships and collaborative practices?

Options:

1. Ask frontline staff what improvements should be made in next year's product models

Developing a Culture of Learning

2. Ensure that senior executives share credit for success at all levels

3. Give employees the opportunity to spend time in a different department one day a month

4. Encourage employees to get feedback from customers and partners

5. Encourage senior executives to treat mistakes as learning experiences

6. Encourage transparency throughout the organization by publishing a monthly newsletter

Answer:

Option 1: This option is correct. Joan should promote equality by getting employees involved in developing product ideas. Egalitarianism involves participation at all levels in the organization.

Option 2: This option is correct. Joan should promote equality by ensuring employees get the credit they deserve. Egalitarianism involves power sharing at all levels in the organization.

Option 3: This option is correct. Joan should encourage people in different departments to collaboratively exchange information and learn from each other. Arranging cross-departmental visits is one way to achieve this.

Option 4: This option is correct. Joan should encourage people to get feedback from people inside and outside the organization. A lot of organizational information is in people's heads, and reaching out to others increases collaborative learning.

Option 5: This option is incorrect. This action encourages employees to view mistakes as learning experiences, which promotes the freedom to experiment and explore, not collaboration or egalitarian relationships.

Option 6: This option is incorrect. This action encourages transparency in the organization, which fosters the freedom to explore, not collaboration or egalitarian relationships.

Case Study: Question 3 of 3

Why should Joan establish egalitarian relationships and collaborative practices?

Options:

1. To open up communication between different levels of seniority

2. To generate events where information is created and shared

3. To increase the likelihood of keeping information confidential

4. To make it easier for people to learn from their mistakes

Answer:

Option 1: This option is correct. Egalitarianism improves communication to allow people to learn from each other. It also reinforces a sense of safety, trust, and fairness in the organization.

Option 2: This option is correct. Collaboration generates events where information is shared between people. It also creates the tensions that motivate people to learn.

Option 3: This option is incorrect. Egalitarian relationships or collaborative practices don't increase the likelihood of keeping information confidential. They promote information sharing where appropriate.

Developing a Culture of Learning

Option 4: This option is incorrect. While egalitarianism and collaboration may make people feel more secure in taking risks, a habit of reflection is required for people to learn from the results of their mistakes.

The importance of motivation

Have you ever met people who are free to explore, collaborate, and learn in an open environment but still don't learn? Perhaps they're not motivated. The motivation to learn is the final and most important condition supporting a learning culture. Motivation is the stimulation that moves a person to work toward a desired goal.

But there are obstacles to motivation. One major obstacle against learning is inertia – the tendency for things and people to stay as they are. How do you overcome this tendency and inspire the motivation to learn and grow?

Question

Why do you think motivation is so important to organizational learning?

Options:

1. Learning is largely self-directed
2. Motivation doesn't cost much

3. Motivation is easy to implement

Answer:

Option 1: This is the correct option. Motivation is important because organizational learning depends on learners taking ownership for and directing their own learning. If people are enthusiastic, they'll learn more effectively.

Option 2: This option is incorrect. Motivation may be free, but that's not why it's important for learning. Motivation is important because learning is largely self-directed.

Option 3: This option is incorrect. It's not always easy to motivate, but it's critical to do so because learning is often self-directed in an organization. It depends on the motivation of learners.

Motivation is important because organizational learning depends to a large extent on learners taking responsibility for their own learning and growth. If your organization is a place where people are motivated and encouraged to think in new ways, they'll be likely to learn and grow.

There's a feedback loop between learning and motivation. Motivation enhances learning – motivated people want to learn and improve. In turn, learning enhances motivation to learn – people who learn want to learn more.

Take the case of a junior clerk who wants to learn and develop new skills. She signs up for extra training courses offered in her field. These stimulate her interest in learning more, which motivates her to take more advanced training courses and even college courses.

Sorin Dumitrascu

Within two years, her training qualifications have helped her to get promoted to manager.

What motivates people to learn

What motivates people? Three common motivators in the workplace are competence, relatedness, and autonomy.

See each motivator to learn more about it.

Competence

As a motivator, competence is the feeling of being confident, responsible, and proud of your work.

Relatedness

Relatedness is the sense of belonging to a group, and taking pleasure in social interaction with others.

Autonomy

Autonomy is the sense of being in charge of your own actions and decisions. It relates to the need for people to chart their own learning path.

People who are motivated by competence need to feel effective in dealing with their environment. They want to feel good at handling problems and issues in the workplace.

They see themselves as learners who can change their skills, understanding, and behaviors.

Consider the case of an accountant who is transferred to the Sales Department. He takes pride in achieving work goals and feels motivated by new challenges, problem solving, and learning new aspects of the business. Changing departments reinforces his motivation to learn because it requires him to figure out how to succeed in a new environment.

People who are motivated by relatedness work best in an environment that fosters collaborative learning. They like to work with and learn from others. Trust and mutual respect also help to set the stage for learning.

Think about this scenario. An engineer transfers into the Sales Department and is assigned to work on customer accounts. Because of the company's collaborative environment, he's able to quickly access the information he needs.

He learns some key things about his new job from people in his new department. Their willingness to share makes him feel like a valued team member already. He learns about products his customers have bought, customer issues, and best practices for customer presentations. He learns quickly, because forging connections between people is second nature to him.

When people have autonomy to decide for themselves how and when they learn, they typically get better results.

Rather than being locked into training programs, many learners prefer to take control of their development, choosing modes of learning that work best for them. Some may prefer informal online research, while others appreciate the chance to ask questions and work with a mentor.

Workplace motivators can be intrinsic or extrinsic. Intrinsic motivators are internal and extrinsic ones are external. Competence, relatedness, and autonomy are intrinsic motivators.

See each type of motivator to learn more about it.

Intrinsic motivators

Intrinsic motivators are innate or inborn. They're connected with personal interest and satisfaction. For example, people's need for recognition and self-esteem are intrinsic motivators.

Extrinsic motivators

Extrinsic motivators come from external sources, and are typically related to reward, punishment, or compliance with rules. For example, a pay increase or job promotion are extrinsic motivators. Extrinsic motivators don't suit workplace learning because they make learners less likely to take ownership of, and engage with, learning. They encourage learners to be passive, rather than self-directed in their learning. At worst, there's a danger that learners may have more interest in the external stimulus than in the learning itself.

Question

Classify each motivator by matching it to its type. Each type may have more than one match.

Options:

A. The need to adapt to a new technology
B. Self-confidence
C. A bonus for good performance
D. Feeling like part of a team

Targets:

1. Intrinsic
2. Extrinsic

Answer:

Intrinsic motivators are innate or inborn. They are connected with personal interest and satisfaction.

Extrinsic motivators come from external sources, often related to rewards or punishments. Extrinsic motivators don't optimize workplace learning.

Motivation: recognition and teamwork

As a leader, you can use four strategies to enhance the motivation to learn in your organization: provide recognition of learning and improvement
- make people feel like part of a team,
- focus on the uniqueness of individuals, and
- provide autonomy and participation.

The first strategy to enhance motivation for learning is to provide recognition of employees' learning abilities, efforts, and successes.

Praising your employees for their learning efforts helps to deepen their appetite for learning because they know their learning is valued.

Recognition could take the form of acknowledging that someone's initiative to learn more about cloud computing has made him the departmental expert. Another example would be letting someone know how her persistence in figuring out how to solve a customer problem has benefited the whole team.

The second strategy to enhance motivation for learning is to fulfill the relatedness motivator by making people feel like they're part of a team.

You can do this by providing opportunities for people to collaborate as they contribute to common goals.

For people to feel they belong, they must feel that their contributions are valued by the team. You can promote this feeling by making each person on a team responsible for different activities, and by ensuring that everyone's ideas are heard and considered by the team.

Question

Which actions are likely to motivate people to learn and grow?

Options:

1. Acknowledging the training programs completed by an engineer in an e-mail to everyone in the Engineering Department

2. Encouraging the members of a customer support team to share what they know about a new process with other team members

3. Giving time off to employees who reach a training milestone

4. Making sure that the planning for all learning initiatives is in the control of the training manager

Answer:

Option 1: This is a correct option. Publicly praising an employee who seeks learning through training is an example of the strategy to provide recognition. This is a way to show confidence in people's ability to learn.

Option 2: This option is correct. Getting people to learn from each other is an example of the strategy of making people feel like they're part of a team. People often want to feel they're part of a group.

Option 3: This option is incorrect. Rewarding employees for taking training isn't an example of a strategy to motivate learning. This is an extrinsic motivator, which will not motivate people to improve and grow, though it might temporarily motivate them to attend the training.

Option 4: This option is incorrect. Restricting planning to the training manager isn't an example of a strategy to motivate learning. Giving the manager control takes away autonomy from employees, and autonomy is a motivator.

Motivation: uniqueness and autonomy

The third strategy to enhance motivation is to focus on the uniqueness of individuals. Your people are individuals who want to learn in their own way. So you'll need to understand people's learning preferences – their preferred learning style and learning delivery mode.

Learning style is the way people like to learn. For example, some people like to learn by solving problems. Others prefer concepts to be explained and demonstrated. Learning delivery mode is the method and situation in which learning takes place. Some modes include e-learning, simulation, role play, or classroom learning, for example.

It's important you tap into individuals' style and delivery preferences and demonstrate that their personal fulfillment in learning is important to you and the organization.

Providing autonomy and participation is the fourth strategy to enhance motivation. When people can decide how and when they learn, they're more motivated to learn. Most people value, and are motivated by, the freedom to pursue their own learning ideas.

Encourage people to participate in determining learning strategies and tactics. Again, people are more driven to learn when they have input into learning decisions.

For example, a manager gives employees the freedom to design how their department will learn a new customer management procedure. Staff members design a learning plan that suits their needs using a combination of on-the-job training, classroom training, follow-up practice, and coaching. Each learning event is marked by a sense of enthusiasm because employees have taken ownership of the program and its results.

Motivation strategies in action

Consider Virginia, the sales manager for a car components manufacturer. The company is diversifying into truck components. She's concerned that her sales team doesn't want to learn new sales techniques for this line of business.

Virginia is trying to get one of her team leads, Eugene, motivated to learn new sales techniques. Follow along as they discuss ways to learn.

Virginia: You know this move into trucks is huge for us...

Virginia is slightly concerned.

Eugene: I know, it's big...

Eugene is agreeing.

Virginia: We have to get better at pitching to that market.

Virginia is concerned.

Eugene: Well, we already know how to sell, and we're just too busy this quarter to train on new techniques.

Developing a Culture of Learning

Eugene is anxious.
Virginia: Really? Remember last year? How easily your team picked up the industry standard techniques? We were swamped then too, but you managed to work it in, and everyone's stats went up.
Virginia is enthusiastic.
Eugene: Yeah, we did well with that.
Eugene is thoughtful.
Virginia: Maybe break it down this time – each team member learns an area of the truck market, then role plays an approach for everyone else.
Virginia is enthusiastic.
Eugene: That might work...
Eugene is enthusiastic.
Virginia: There would have to be a few classroom-based sessions too...
Virginia is thoughtful.
Eugene: Any way to make those more portable – to fit in between sales calls?
Eugene is doubtful.
Virginia: Could be an e-learning alternative. I'll check with the rest of the team to get their preferences.
Virginia is cheerful.
Eugene: OK...oh, and next month we're all attending those trade shows...
Eugene is agreeing.
Virginia: Absolutely! I'll let everyone plan their own training around the shows.
Virginia is happy.
Eugene: I'll start on my own plan right away.
Eugene is happy.
Question

Match the motivational strategies Virginia used with the statements that represent them.

Options:

A. Provide recognition
B. Make people feel like part of a team
C. Focus on the uniqueness of individuals
D. Provide autonomy and participation

Targets:

1. "Remember last year? How easily your team picked up the industry standard techniques?"
2. "Maybe break it down this time – each team member learns an area, then role plays an approach for everyone else."
3. "I'll check with the rest of the team to get their preferences."
4. "I'll let everyone plan their own training around the shows."

Answer:

Providing recognition helps to express confidence in your people's competence and ability to learn.

Making people feel part of a team involves giving opportunities for them to interact with others.

Focusing on the uniqueness of individuals and accommodating their learning preferences motivates people to learn in their own way.

Providing autonomy motivates people by giving them ownership over their own learning decisions.

In her conversation, Virginia motivated her team members in different ways. She provided recognition of Eugene's past learning efforts and made him feel like part of a team by encouraging collaborative role play. She also recognized the uniqueness of individuals by catering to individuals' training preferences. Last, Virginia gave team members the autonomy to decide their own training schedule.

Many leaders do a good job of providing the resources and programs that enable people to learn. But enabling is not enough – employees need to be empowered as well. The actions you take to create a learning culture will help to empower employees to learn, grow, and flourish. These actions should be sustained as employees continue to learn into the future.

Using strategies for motivation

You've examined a number of strategies to empower people and enhance the motivation to learn in your organization. You'll now have an opportunity to practice recognizing these strategies in action.

Case Study: Question 1 of 2

Scenario

Follow along as Lucy, the finance VP, discusses opportunities to learn at an upcoming share trading conference with one of her reports, Alex.

Lucy: So, are you looking forward to the share trading conference next week?

Lucy is enthusiastic.

Alex: Yeah – there'll be people there from every major player in our business.

Alex is enthusiastic.

Lucy: I'm sure you'll learn lots. Remember that audit conference? You learned so much, you're now our number one audit guy!

Developing a Culture of Learning

Lucy is enthusiastic.

Alex: Yeah – I guess it will be good to know more about share trading.

Alex is eager.

Lucy: Here's the real benefit: after the conference you can bring back what you know. We'll all look to you for the latest thinking on legal issues.

Lucy is enthusiastic.

Alex: Well, I'd better take good notes, then!

Alex is sincere.

Question

What strategies to motivate learning did Lucy use in her discussion with Alex?

Options:

1. Providing recognition of learning and improvement
2. Making people feel like part of a team
3. Focusing on the uniqueness of individuals
4. Providing autonomy and participation

Answer:

Option 1: This option is correct. Lucy provided recognition by reminding Alex of his previous learning success.

Option 2: This option is correct. Lucy made Alex feel like part of a team by encouraging him to share his newfound legal knowledge. Most people want to be valued as part of a group.

Option 3: This option is incorrect. Lucy's discussion didn't focus on Alex's unique learning styles or preferences.

Option 4: This option is incorrect. Lucy didn't specifically give Alex control or autonomy over his learning effort in this scenario.

Case Study: Question 2 of 2

What else could Lucy do to increase Alex's motivation to learn and grow?

Options:

1. Get him to learn about share trading by adapting training to suit his individual learning preferences
2. Tell him to come up with his own learning schedule for the share trading conference
3. Tell him to follow a centralized learning plan for the conference
4. Tell him that the budget for the share trading conference is reduced by 20%

Answer:

Option 1: This option is correct. Adapting training to suit different learning styles would motivate Alex because it focuses on him as an individual.

Option 2: This option is correct. Letting Alex devise the learning schedule would encourage his autonomy and involvement. Most people like the freedom to pursue their own learning efforts.

Option 3: This option is incorrect. Following a centralized learning plan doesn't increase motivation. However, adapting courses to different learning styles motivates learning.

Option 4: This option is incorrect. Telling Alex about budget cuts doesn't increase motivation.

CHAPTER THREE
Developing Learning Practices

Supporting a learning culture

Many people view life as one long learning curve. They see opportunities to improve their knowledge and skills as their lives progress. Organizations have also adopted this approach by fostering a strong learning culture for employees.

To create a learning culture in your own organization, you can introduce practices that support learning initiatives. Organizational learning involves four practices: planning for learning, building knowledge, diffusing knowledge, and applying knowledge.

In organizations with strong learning cultures, learning will often occur spontaneously during work activities. It's important, however, to engage in planning as well. Planning for learning involves carrying out assessments of employees' learning needs. Conducting a needs assessment will help ensure that learning activities align with the learning needs of the employees and with the strategic goals and priorities of the organization.

Developing a Culture of Learning

Question

How would you rate your organization's ability to carry out a needs assessment as part of the planning for learning process?

Options:

1. Very competent
2. Competent
3. Not very competent

Answer:

Option 1: Great! You rate your organization as being very competent at carrying out a needs assessment. You might find some new and useful ideas in the rest of this topic that you can bring back to your organization.

Option 2: You rate your organization as being competent at carrying out a needs assessment. This is a good position to be in. You might find some new ideas that may add to your organization's ability to plan for learning.

Option 3: You rate your organization as being not very competent at carrying out needs assessments as part of planning for learning. The rest of this topic will provide you with ideas and suggestions to help you to improve your organization's ability in this area.

Conducting a learning needs assessment will help identify areas where your organization needs improvement to remain competitive. It contributes to employee buy-in and prioritizes the use of learning interventions. There are three steps for conducting a learning needs assessment. The first step is to define and prioritize development needs. The second step is to collect data. The third and final step is to analyze results.

Defining development needs

Defining development needs is the first step for conducting a learning needs assessment. As a leader, you use this step to determine what level the organization needs to function at.

You do this by identifying desired conditions for success. This includes recognizing opportunities to act upon and knowing what resources you need and why you need them.

These different elements give you an indication of what your organization should do to foster a strong learning culture.

A development need occurs when a person is able to perform a task but currently lacks the knowledge or skills to do it to a high standard. Development needs can be identified from a number of different sources:

- market opportunities the organization plans to capitalize on,

- impending changes in the market or regulatory landscape,
- problems or deficits in the organization,
- current strengths that could be spread to other areas of the organization, and
- organizational strategy.

See each potential source from which development needs can be identified to learn more about it.

Market opportunities

Market opportunities can range from moving into new markets to capitalizing on a gap in the current market.

For example, management of a beverage company wants to push a product into an emerging market where this type of beverage is currently unavailable. The managers identify a development need of providing some of the company's sales and marketing employees with training about product expansion into foreign territories.

The company also identifies an opportunity to capitalize on a gap in the current market when one of its competitors goes out of business. The company wants to produce a sports drink to fill the gap. Management identifies a development need to provide employees with training about producing sports drinks.

Impending changes

An organization may need to do something different that requires its employees to learn new skills or behaviors in reaction to a market or regulatory change.

Take a chemical manufacturer, for instance. A development need is identified because new regulations are introduced governing the disposal of chemical waste products. Some of the company's employees will need to receive training about the new legislation.

Problems or deficits

Leaders will analyze their organizations to find weaknesses. They will introduce improvements that need to be made in order for their organizations to perform better, faster, and smarter. Implementing these improvements can create development needs.

For instance, an online retailer's customer service call center receives very poor ratings in a performance evaluation. Customers were dissatisfied with the time it took to handle queries and rated the customer service operators' knowledge of the retailer's online system as very poor. The company realizes that further training needs to be provided for employees in the call center.

Current strengths

Another source of development needs is when an organization's current strengths are assessed to determine if they can be spread to other areas of the organization.

For example, a computer hardware manufacturer's sales team has developed its own method for quickly dealing with invoices. The company's management considers if the skills the sales team has developed can be applied to the Procurement Department so that purchase orders can be dealt with in a similarly prompt way.

Organizational strategy

Organizations create strategic plans that provide direction for the future.

For instance, as part of its organizational strategy, a marketing company wants to capitalize on all emerging social media platforms. The company wants to position itself as an innovative company in its industry. The development need in this case is to provide employees with the skills necessary to manipulate social media for marketing purposes.

Development needs shouldn't be confused or combined with personal issues, process issues, or equipment issues. A personal issue can involve an individual being unwilling or unable to perform a task. A process issue is where the process isn't functioning properly and needs to be changed. An equipment issue is when equipment becomes outdated or no longer works.

When you define development needs, be aware that the relationship between strategy and learning is evolving. Traditionally, an organization would analyze market conditions and develop a strategic plan first. It would then train and qualify the workforce to implement the strategy.

Increasingly, the strategy and learning functions have developed a symbiotic relationship that no longer includes taking separate, structured step-by-step planning approaches.

Question

Kathy is a manager with a large food processing company. She is responsible for developing organizational learning throughout the company. She identifies several challenges in her organization.

Which challenges represent development needs?

Options:

1. Increase the sales team's knowledge of current nutritional trends globally to boost sales

2. Provide the audit team with upskilling because of changes to tax regulations

3. Enable the IT Department to react faster to virus threats

4. Apply the working methods of a successful unit to a less successful unit

5. Instigate lean initiatives outlined by the company's strategy

6. Change the processes on equipment use

7. Develop motivational training initiatives for employees who are currently underperforming

Answer:

Option 1: This option is correct. The company has identified certain nutritional trends that are becoming important for consumers worldwide. Boosting the sales team's knowledge of these trends is a development need derived from market opportunity.

Option 2: This option is correct. Introducing new training to deal with changes in tax regulations is a development need arising from impending changes in the market or regulatory landscape.

Option 3: This option is correct. The company identifies a development need because of a problem or deficit in relation to the IT Department's ability to deal with virus threats.

Option 4: This option is correct. Analyzing where a company's current strengths could be spread to other parts of the company can generate development needs.

Option 5: This option is correct. A company's organizational strategy is one source of development needs.

Option 6: This option is incorrect. Process and equipment issues aren't challenges that represent development needs.

Option 7: This option is incorrect. A personal issue doesn't represent a development need.

Collecting data

The second step when conducting a learning needs assessment is to collect data. During this step you find out what employees know and don't know, as well as what they can and can't do. This step will identify the knowledge within your organization in terms of your workforce's ability to contribute to organizational goals. You will also be able to identify where this knowledge exists. In turn, you can pinpoint where there are knowledge gaps that hinder your organization's effectiveness.

The main purpose of collecting data is to find out what your workforce needs to know. Completing this step will help you to identify each individual's starting point or current state. In other words, you discover the person's baseline knowledge and skills.

As you conduct your data collection activities, you should try to learn about the individuals themselves. By gaining insight into their personal opinions, needs, styles, and preferences, you can tailor your learning interventions so that they effectively help those who need them most.

To accurately assess a learning need, you should break it down into its individual components. For example, say you have identified a learning need within your organization to improve employees' knowledge of Enterprise Resource Planning, or ERP, software.

First you identify what employees currently know. Then you find out where the major knowledge gaps exist.

You focus on these gaps and seek to create a learning program that will boost knowledge and skills in these areas.

Your response may have listed some of these tools for assessing an employee's current state: interviews, questionnaires, and focus groups. Each tool will be discussed in greater detail, starting with conducting interviews.

Interviews

Conducting interviews is an effective way of gathering information from employees. Carol is a manager of research and development with a pharmaceutical company. She is interviewing Ellen, a research scientist who works in her department. Follow along as Carol gathers information from Ellen.

Carol: Hi Ellen. You know I'm speaking to everyone on the team about learning needs in the company.

Carol is pleasant and engaging.

Ellen: Sure.

Ellen is friendly.

Carol: So, let's start with the new legislative compliance issues. You know they're coming soon. How do you think they'll affect your role?

Carol is friendly.

Ellen: Well, I'm a research scientist, right? I'm always mindful of compliance and obviously any testing of products has to be carried out ethically. But from a research perspective, I don't think these issues'll have a huge influence on how I do my job.

Ellen is friendly and enthusiastic.

Carol: But testing's a crucial part of your job, isn't it? And the new regulations seem to be pretty restrictive.

Carol is friendly.

Ellen: You might be right. But what drives me is biotechnology research to create new and more effective vaccines. What if my research comes to nothing because I can't prove I'm in compliance with the new legislation?

Ellen is impulsive.

Carol: Ellen, your research can't be used by the company unless it's in compliance with new legislation. And being in compliance is the only way to get your new vaccines to the public!

Carol is friendly.

Ellen: I see your point.

Ellen is chastened.

Carol: Do you think a training session focused on testing under the new legislation would be useful?

Carol is supportive.

Ellen: Yes. But the more focused the training can be on testing the better...

Ellen is confident and rather serious.

Carol : Sure.

Carol is friendly.

Carol used the interview to ask Ellen if she knew how the compliance issues would affect her role. In addition, she asked Ellen if she will need training to deal with compliance.

Carol helped Ellen understand the importance of compliance, but she could also have asked Ellen's opinion on where the company could improve on current learning opportunities and if there are areas the company needs to address.

Questionnaires and focus groups

As well as conducting interviews, there are two other tools of use for assessing an employee's current state. Questionnaires and focus groups are both effective when used in the proper circumstances.

See each remaining tool for assessing an employee's current state to learn more about it.

Questionnaires

Questionnaires can be used to gather specific information about an individual's knowledge gaps. They can also be used to collate information on an organization's overall learning and development needs.

When you're creating your questionnaire you should use closed-ended questions if you want to generate statistical information. Here's an example of a closed-ended question: "How many accredited hours of training have you undertaken in advance welding techniques this year?"

To gather qualitative information from a questionnaire, open-ended questions are more suitable. This is an example of an open-ended question: "What's your opinion of the learning opportunities the firm has provided in relation to best practices in human resources management?"

Focus groups

Focus groups bring together a range of employees from within an organization. Their discussion helps develop a holistic view of addressing areas where learning needs exist.

A focus group asks participants to collectively reflect on and discuss issues relating to learning needs. Some focus groups introduce a visual element in the form of organizational charts so that participants can see the learning needs for each part of the organization. Participants can draw connections and see where learning needs overlap. This method also allows participants to make suggestions and to simulate outcomes.

In addition, other tools such as testing and quality monitoring can be used for assessment. Testing occurs when an employee's ability to carry out a job, task, or process is assessed to determine if a learning need exists. Testing is time consuming but will provide a clear indication of whether or not there is a knowledge gap. Quality monitoring involves reviewing error rates and performance reports. The trends and patterns that emerge may reveal knowledge gaps in an organization.

Question

Kathy, the manager responsible for developing organizational learning in a food processing company, is now collecting data for a learning needs assessment.

What are the appropriate activities Kathy should undertake to collect data?

Options:

1. Use a questionnaire to discover how much employees know about food hygiene

2. Interview employees in the Testing Department to discover what skills they possess that relate
  specifically to their work with the company

3. Ask members of the ingredients preparation team to take part in a focus group

4. Ask employees an open-ended question to gather statistical information

5. Carry out testing to quickly learn what learning needs exist in the company

Answer:

Option 1: This option is correct. Questionnaires can be used to gather specific information about an individual's knowledge gaps. They can also be used to collate information on an organization's overall learning and development needs.

Option 2: This option is correct. Interviews are an effective tool for gathering specific information in relation to an employee's learning needs.

Option 3: This option is correct. Focus groups ask participants to collectively reflect on and discuss issues relating to learning needs.

Option 4: This option is incorrect. You should use a closed-ended question to gather statistical information.

Option 5: This option is incorrect. Testing is a very time consuming way to collect data.

Analyzing results

The third step for conducting a learning needs assessment is to analyze the results of the data you collected in the previous step. Analyzing the results involves identifying gaps, looking for trends, comparing costs and benefits, checking compatibility with strategic goals, and determining priorities.

Identifying gaps is the first element of analyzing the results. Once the data has been collected and the results revealed, you can then look for knowledge gaps in the organization.

For example, Simon is the manager at a publishing company. After studying the results from data collected, he identifies that his sales team doesn't feel comfortable dealing with electronic publishing platforms such as e-readers.

The second element of analyzing results is to look for trends in the data. You should pinpoint instances where patterns emerge. This can highlight if there's a systematic learning failure across the organization. For instance, Emily is a training supervisor with a management consultancy firm. She discovers a trend showing that employees who are with the company for three years or less all display a deficit of knowledge about how to headhunt managerial talent.

Comparing costs and benefits is another aspect of analyzing results. It involves examining urgency and exploring the consequences of implementing or not implementing a learning development initiative.

See each aspect relating to comparing costs and benefits to learn more about it.

Examining urgency

When you identify learning needs, you then have to assess their urgency. Does the need require immediate attention or can it wait? For example, the learning need may affect a customer's order that is due. Or the learning need may relate to a change in legislation that won't be implemented for six months.

Exploring consequences

After identifying a learning need, you should consider the implication of launching the development program versus not launching it. For example, if the learning need is significant, the consequence of launching a development program could be that production will slow down in the short term, but overall productivity will increase over time. However, if you don't launch it, production will remain at a steady rate, but productivity will never increase.

You should check that your learning development program is compatible with strategic goals. Some learning development programs may not align with the organization's strategy.

For example, Omar is the CEO of an electronic goods manufacturer. A learning need is identified in the company's R&D team. The R&D personnel need to learn more about designing attractive kitchen appliances.

However, the company has implemented a strategy to focus entirely on producing goods for the home entertainment market. Omar realizes that launching a skills development program focusing on domestic appliances would be incompatible with the company's strategy.

You determine which development needs you should prioritize based on the gaps and trends that you've identified. You also take into consideration the identified development need's compatibility with the organization's strategy and the findings from your cost benefit analysis.

Question

From what you have learned so far, what do you think are the benefits of conducting a learning needs assessment?

Options:

1. It reveals the knowledge you have in the organization
2. It promotes buy-in from employees
3. It helps prioritize areas for learning interventions
4. It will reduce the organization's expenditure on upskilling and training
5. It will benefit employees at the executive and management levels only

Answer:

Option 1: This option is correct. Identifying this knowledge makes it available for use and transmission to other areas in the organization that could benefit from it.

Option 2: This option is correct. A learning needs assessment promotes buy-in from employees by involving them in the process of learning. When people have input as to how and what they will learn, they will generally feel more invested when the learning program is unveiled.

Option 3: This option is correct. Once a learning needs assessment has been successfully completed, you will have documented evidence to support the implementation of learning interventions in areas where employees have specific knowledge gaps.

Option 4: This option is incorrect. The purpose of a learning needs assessment isn't solely to discover areas where an organization can create savings.

Option 5: This option is incorrect. A learning needs assessment is designed to benefit all stakeholders at every level throughout the organization, not just the executive and management levels.

After you have completed your needs assessment process, you document your learning strategy in a plan. This plan sets the direction for your learning initiative.

The plan outlines why it should be implemented, how it will be implemented, the time line for implementation, and the expected outcomes.

Question

Kathy, the manager responsible for developing organizational learning in a food processing company, is now analyzing the results of the needs assessment to prepare the learning strategy.

Which methods should she use to analyze these results?

Developing a Culture of Learning

Options:
1. She should use the data to identify knowledge deficits
2. She should identify patterns in the data
3. She should compare the pros and cons of addressing a learning need
4. She should check the learning need's strategic compatibility
5. She should prioritize needs based on gaps, compatibility, consequences, and trends
6. She should initiate a development need based on her instincts
7. She should use cost to prioritize needs

Answer:
Option 1: This option is correct. Identifying gaps in knowledge is an element of analyzing results.

Option 2: This option is correct. Identifying patterns and trends is part of analyzing the results.

Option 3: This option is correct. Comparing the consequences of launching a development need program is an element of analyzing the results.

Option 4: This option is correct. Checking a development need's compatibility with strategy is an element of analyzing results.

Option 5: This option is correct. Determining priorities after taking gaps and trends in the data into account, as well as making comparisons and checking compatibility, is the final element of analyzing results.

Option 6: This option is incorrect. Using instinct to make a decision doesn't involve any analysis of results.

Option 7: This option is incorrect. Costs and benefits should be compared when prioritizing needs.

Building knowledge in an organization

When an organization's management decides to foster a learning culture for its employees, it must consider how to build knowledge in the organization. Building knowledge is the second practice that relates to organizational learning.

After a learning needs assessment has been completed, an organization considers what learning interventions and tools it might use to address the lack of knowledge the assessment identifies. These include running in-house conferences about the latest research developments and creating training programs. Other approaches include developing instructional DVDs and organizing coaching sessions.

There are two different approaches to building knowledge in a company or organization. The first is to acquire it. The second approach is to create it.

See each method for building knowledge to learn more about it.

Acquire it

Acquiring knowledge involves identifying and then accessing sources of knowledge from inside and outside your organization. This acquired knowledge is then used to expand the abilities of one or more individuals within the organization.

Create it

You can create knowledge by developing new and innovative ideas for the organization. This process creates new knowledge that can be disseminated to any area in the organization that requires it. You can create knowledge from within by establishing expert teams that can share their findings with colleagues.

Both acquiring and creating knowledge are integral to any learning initiative. You should take the needs and characteristics of your particular workforce into account when you decide how much of each approach you are going to use.

Acquiring knowledge

The first method you can use to build knowledge within your organization is acquiring knowledge. There are many internal sources that an organization can access to acquire knowledge. This includes accessing the diverse skills of its workforce. People with expert skills pass their knowledge along.

For example, knowledge can be acquired through shared visioning and mental modeling. These activities tap into an organization's know-how. Shared visioning involves brainstorming sessions and swapping ideas. Employees create mental models by analyzing every detail relating to an issue, including causes and consequences.

Team learning is another internal source of knowledge. The findings or results generated by a team involved in a learning initiative can be made available to everyone in the organization.

Organizations can also use external sources to acquire knowledge. These include the latest up-to-date industry publications, peer-reviewed best practices, market research firms, industry experts' recommendations, and reports from consulting companies.

Growing an individual's knowledge in an organization is part of the acquisition process and involves many activities:

- taking on new assignments and projects,
- self-directed learning using internal and external sources,
- shadowing,
- mentoring, and
- Training.

See each activity that can be used to help grow an individual's knowledge to learn more about it.

Taking on new assignments

Encouraging individuals to take on new assignments and projects creates a sustained approach to learning. The individuals are challenged by the tasks they're taking on. They'll have to push themselves and in some cases learn new competencies and skills to be successful.

For example, a cell phone manufacturer requires that all of its research engineers complete a project related to an area they don't have much experience in.

Self-directed learning

Self-directed learning is when employees use their own initiative to improve their knowledge. It involves accessing internal and external sources.

For instance, a marketing executive working for a soft drink company collects and analyzes industry reports to learn about emerging trends.

Shadowing

Shadowing is a form of action learning. This type of learning is used when a person has acquired new knowledge and now wants to know how to put theory into practice. An employee follows and observes an experienced colleague in the workplace. The employee's ability to perform the same task should improve as a result.

In this example, Larry – an assembly line supervisor for a car manufacturer – shadows Marvin, a line manager, so that he can learn how best to use his newly learned people-management skills.

Mentoring

Mentoring is another form of action learning. An employee has acquired a new level of knowledge and wants to apply it to a role in the workplace. To do so, a more experienced colleague is assigned to provide encouragement and assistance.

For example, Steve is a lab technician working for a medical research firm. He has learned new skills about testing samples that have been exposed to high temperatures. Grace, a more experienced technician, mentors Steve as he begins to use his new skills.

Training

For training to be successful, a company must explain to the individual why the content needs to be learned, what the objectives are, how success will be measured, and how the training will be delivered. The individual's knowledge of the subject should increase once the instruction is provided in concise chunks and there's an opportunity to complete unguided practice with feedback.

In this example, Matthew is an owner of a software company. He explains to Lisa, a member of his sales

Developing a Culture of Learning

team, that she needs to receive training in how the company's payroll software product works so that she can explain the product's selling points to potential customers. A member of the programming team will provide the instruction and rate how well Lisa is able to use the software to accomplish a series of payroll-related tasks.

Question

Which examples represent activities that will help grow an individual's knowledge?

Options:

1. An electronics company discourages employees from taking on new initiatives

2. An accountancy firm's employees only undertake learning initiatives if asked to do so

3. A statistical analysis company creates a shadowing program to help employees understand how to use their new skills

4. A telecommunications firm uses a mentoring approach to help employees apply what they've learned to their roles

5. An engineering company outlines the purpose of its employee training program

Answer:

Option 1: This option is incorrect. Encouraging individuals to take on new assignments and projects helps them acquire knowledge and creates a sustained approach to learning.

Option 2: This option is incorrect. Employees should be encouraged to undertake self-directed learning to acquire knowledge.

Option 3: This option is correct. Shadowing is a form of action learning. It's a way to acquire knowledge and should help improve employees' abilities to perform a task.

Option 4: This option is correct. Mentoring helps an employee who has acquired a new level of knowledge to apply it to a role in the workplace.

Option 5: This option is correct. Training is an effective way to grow individual knowledge. For training to be successful, a company must explain to the individual why the content needs to be learned, what the objectives are, how success will be measured, and how the training will be delivered.

Facilitating knowledge acquisition

Leaders and managers facilitate knowledge acquisition in the workplace by implementing several initiatives. They instill a sense of ownership and responsibility for individual learning; promote collaboration; provide rewards and recognition for learning; tailor interventions to individuals and situations; and integrate learning with the job.

The first way to facilitate knowledge acquisition is to instill a sense of ownership and responsibility for individual learning. Asking employees to take active control of their learning journey results in a greater level of buy-in to the process.

Employees are likely to react more positively if they have some control over the learning process. They will be more engaged and open to learning new skills.

For example, a telecommunications company asks its employees to contribute proposals for inclusion in its learning strategy. Many employees express an interest in developing their skills in relation to improving software that allows users to make voice and video calls over the Internet. When the learning initiatives are implemented, the response from the workforce is very positive.

Promoting collaboration is another important method of facilitating knowledge acquisition. As a leader you should try to encourage people to work together to build new mindsets and develop knowledge throughout your organization.

You can achieve this by putting individuals in a position to learn from each other. When motivated employees are put in this position, they'll encourage each other to learn.

Take Yasmine, for example. She is the manager of an insurance company's customer service section. Whenever a learning need about premium calculation is identified, she uses the collaborative approach to training. Her team is then able to acquire the knowledge needed by drawing on the knowledge levels of team members who have experience in calculating premiums.

Providing rewards and recognition for learning is another way to facilitate knowledge acquisition in the workplace. To become a learning organization, you should provide recognition to encourage all employees to continually learn.

Ideally, employees will have a proactive approach to learning. This means that they undertake training to adapt to a change that they're willing to make, rather than reacting to a change they have to make. However, you will sometimes need to create incentives for employees to become proactive learners.

For instance, a finance company provides incentives to encourage its employees to embrace learning opportunities. An employee who completes a minor learning initiative is mentioned in the company newsletter. When an employee completes a major learning initiative, the person may qualify for a salary increase.

Question

What facilitates knowledge acquisition?

Options:

1. Encouraging employees to take control of their own learning development

2. Advocating that employees collaborate on learning initiatives

3. Rewarding employees who complete learning initiatives

4. Concentrating on using internal sources to acquire knowledge

5. Encouraging employees to focus on external sources to acquire knowledge

Answer:

Option 1: This option is correct. Asking employees to take active control of their learning journey results in a greater level of buy-in to the process.

Option 2: This option is correct. When motivated employees collaborate on learning initiatives, they'll encourage each other to learn.

Option 3: This option is correct. Providing rewards creates incentives for employees to acquire knowledge.

Option 4: This option is incorrect. Organizations should use internal and external sources to acquire knowledge.

Option 5: This option is incorrect. Both external and internal sources are vital for knowledge acquisition.

Tailoring interventions to individuals and situations also facilitates knowledge acquisition. When you're considering your learning strategy, regard your workforce as a group of individual learners. Each employee will have a certain learning need to deal with a particular situation. Implementing a very broad, one-size-fits-all learning intervention is likely to result in some employees not benefiting to the extent that they need to.

Here's an example of tailoring interventions to individuals and situations. Maria is a human resources administrator with a medium-sized manufacturer of lighting fixtures.

The company hires several temporary employees on short-term contracts. Maria is provided with training that covers the legislation relating to this type of employment contract. She is then able to manage the influx of temporary employees more effectively.

In another example of tailoring interventions, Zack is the owner of a small freight company. After conducting a learning needs assessment, he identifies areas in the company where there's a lack of knowledge. He realizes that unless he tailors the learning interventions, his efforts won't be effective.

Ralph, who's in charge of route planning, needs more training in advanced logistics management. Melanie, who's responsible for the trucks and vans the company uses, requires further training in fleet management.

Zack tailors the learning interventions to suit each individual's learning need in relation to that person's working situation.

The final method for facilitating knowledge acquisition is to integrate learning with the job. You should make it clear to employees that your organization regards learning as an important business process.

Ensure employees realize organizational learning is of equal importance to the production of goods or the delivery of a service. You can make learning a part of daily operations by regarding each function and process as an opportunity to learn and improve.

For instance, a food company's management encourages its employees to view every activity as a learning opportunity. The company's managers explain to employees that it's important to learn as they produce. The employees start recording problems and solutions they encounter in an activity book. This attitude toward learning turns a production system into a learning system also.

Question

Which actions facilitate knowledge acquisition?

Options:

1. An advertising firm asks workers to take ownership of the learning process

2. An accounting company promotes collaborative learning

3. A web design company creates a reward scheme

4. A bank implements learning initiatives on an individual basis

5. A computer hardware company incorporates learning into each process

6. A law firm restricts learning opportunities to specific times during the year

7. A construction company's learning interventions take place off-site

Answer:

Option 1: This option is correct. Asking workers to take ownership of the learning process is a way to instill responsibility for individual learning.

Option 2: This option is correct. Promoting collaborative learning facilitates knowledge acquisition by putting people in a position where they can learn from each other.

Option 3: This option is correct. Creating a reward scheme is a method for recognizing employees' learning efforts. It provides an incentive for them to pursue knowledge.

Option 4: This option is correct. Implementing learning initiatives on an individual basis is part of the tailoring process that matches the learning need to the appropriate learning intervention.

Option 5: This option is correct. Integrating learning with the job is an effective way to facilitate knowledge acquisition.

Option 6: This option is incorrect. Organizations should aim to provide learning opportunities at all times.

Option 7: This option is incorrect. Learning interventions are more effective if they are integrated with daily processes.

Creating knowledge

The second method you can use for building knowledge is creating knowledge. This involves developing innovative ideas. You should try to create organizational environments that encourage innovative ideas.

Here's an example of a learning activity that's designed to create knowledge. A company brings together a large group of its employees who share common work processes.

The Human Resources Department has identified a number of issues that it would like the group to discuss. The larger group is divided into smaller groups and each one is asked to discuss different issues.

In these groups, employees discuss the issues from different perspectives. By combining their collective knowledge, the groups are able to create new solutions. Another benefit of this method is that the people who suggest the solutions will eventually be actively involved in implementing them.

Question

An e-commerce company encourages employees with similar roles to form teams as a way of building knowledge. Does this approach represent acquiring knowledge or creating knowledge?

Options:

1. Acquiring knowledge
2. Creating knowledge

Answer:

Option 1: This option is incorrect. Acquiring knowledge involves taking on new assignments, self-directed learning, job shadowing, job mentoring, and training.

Option 2: This is the correct option. By combining their collective knowledge, the team is able to create new solutions.

As a leader, you can use several different methods to facilitate the creation of knowledge. These include encouraging and rewarding experimentation, recognizing the importance of debate and conflict, promoting cross-fertilization, and ensuring inclusivity.

Encouraging and rewarding experimentation is a great way to facilitate knowledge creation. Experimentation often creates exciting, innovative, and useful knowledge.

You should recognize the value of employees who are willing to take risks and attempt different things. These individuals may try and fail, but they will learn from the process. The feedback from their efforts is knowledge that has been created by their experimentation.

For example, a semiconductor company tries to ensure that all of its departments have at least one employee

Developing a Culture of Learning

who's prepared to experiment and willing to push the boundaries.

As a leader, you should be prepared to recognize the importance of debate and conflict. Disagreements and differences of opinion create fertile ground for learning experiences.

Debate and conflict – when properly handled – can get the best out of people. Innovations and solutions frequently stem from individuals or groups debating the merits of their own points of view.

For instance, a computer tablet manufacturer's design team developed a solution to a product's design flaw. The breakthrough came after several group meetings where the issue was vigorously debated.

Promoting cross-fertilization also helps create knowledge. Cross-fertilization means using new information created in one department of a company and applying it to other departments. For this process to take place, an organization should make information available to all interested parties through learning labs or knowledge networks.

See each approach for making information available to all sections of an organization to learn more about it.

Learning labs

A learning lab, or learning laboratory, is a managerial approach that provides employees with an opportunity to simulate some of the ideas they're developing. The learning lab facilitates the development of model simulations. It also allows learners to slowly reflect on the potential outcomes of decisions being discussed.

Knowledge networks

Knowledge networks are technology-supported repositories of organizational expertise and information. Knowledge networks help spread knowledge throughout an organization. Each network is only as good as the information it contains. Information that's derived from sources such as project workshops, customer surveys, and product testing should be fed into a knowledge network. This information is then readily accessible to all members of the workforce.

For example, a company that produces electronic products for the consumer market uses a knowledge network to help promote cross-fertilization. A group of key stakeholders is assembled to discuss every new product the company develops. The stakeholders come from every area of the company affected by the new product development.

This group includes the marketing manager, a member of the design team, the production manager, a sales representative, and a member of the engineering team. The stakeholders are experts in their own fields. However, they have limited knowledge of other requirements that are needed to move a product's development forward.

The meeting of this group helps to create knowledge and learning, which is documented for other members of the company to use. Members of the group share their expertise to create a higher level of knowledge that can be spread throughout the company.

Ensuring inclusivity is another way to help create knowledge in an organization. Companies should allow employees at all levels to contribute their opinions. Creative thinking isn't solely the responsibility of senior management and decision makers. Often, the most effective and creative solutions are suggested by frontline employees. These employees are closer to the problem and will ultimately have to implement the solution. This means that they're highly motivated to find the right idea.

Here's an example. Managers of a plastics molding company were unable to identify a problem with one of the company's process lines. The finished products weren't meeting the specifications. Management believed the problem lay with the workers on the process line, and so asked these workers for their opinions. One of the workers on the process line suggested that the molding machines' settings should all be canceled and then reset so that they become synchronized. This solution solved the problem.

Case Study: Question 1 of 2
Scenario

For your convenience, the case study is repeated with each question.

A company that produces antivirus software uses a group discussion approach to build knowledge.

Demonstrate your understanding of how to build knowledge in an organization by answering the questions in order.

Question

Does the antivirus software company's approach represent acquiring knowledge or creating knowledge?

Options:
1. Acquiring
2. Creating

Answer:

Using group discussions is a method for creating knowledge. By combining their collective knowledge, a group is able to create new knowledge by finding solutions.

Option 1: This option is incorrect. Acquiring knowledge involves taking on new assignments, self-directed learning, job shadowing, job mentoring, and training.

Option 2: This is the correct option. Using group discussions is a method of creating knowledge. By combining their collective knowledge, a group is able to create new knowledge by finding solutions.

Case Study: Question 2 of 2

What strategies should the antivirus software company use to help create knowledge?

Options:

1. It should welcome experimental approaches to tackling new viruses
2. It should create situations where virus prevention ideas are debated
3. It should use knowledge networks to spread new software programing skills
4. It should welcome creative input about virus detection and prevention from employees at every level
5. It should reward employees for completing learning programs
6. It should tailor learning interventions to suit each individual's specific needs

Answer:

Option 1: This option is correct. Encouraging and rewarding experimentation facilitates knowledge creation. This strategy recognizes the value of employees who are willing to take risks and attempt different things.

Option 2: This option is correct. Situations where ideas are debated or where positive conflict occurs can create fertile ground for learning experiences and the creation of knowledge.

Option 3: This option is correct. Using knowledge networks is a way to promote the cross-fertilization of ideas throughout the company.

Option 4: This option is correct. Welcoming creative input from employees at every level is an example of ensuring inclusivity to facilitate the creation of knowledge.

Option 5: This option is incorrect. Establishing an award scheme for learning is a strategy that is used to facilitate the acquisition of knowledge.

Option 6: This option is incorrect. Tailoring learning interventions to suit an individual's specific needs is a strategy used to facilitate the acquisition of knowledge.

Storing knowledge

Organizations go to considerable lengths to build knowledge by acquiring or creating it. The next task is to diffuse the knowledge throughout the organization to help employees improve their performance. This is the third practice relating to organizational learning.

Diffusing knowledge can help to develop innovations and discover efficiencies. Organizations may lose out if knowledge is housed among a small group of individuals – it should be shared with the entire company.

To successfully diffuse knowledge, you must store it correctly. There's no point in accumulating useful information and then making it difficult to access. Information should be readily available to employees who need to access it. You should give careful consideration to how your organization maintains, stores, and secures knowledge. You can use databases, internal information systems, and knowledge awareness workshops to help maintain and store knowledge.

See each method for maintaining and storing knowledge to learn more about it.

Databases

Databases are an effective tool for storing knowledge. Organizations can easily update and cross-reference information in the database.

Internal information systems

There are many types of internal information systems. Organizations can purchase software to create systems or develop their own systems in-house. These systems can be modified to store information and make it accessible to employees. They also capture and record data that is created from the organization's everyday processes.

Knowledge awareness workshops

Knowledge awareness workshops are used to facilitate knowledge transfer. The workshops are usually held after a period of intense knowledge building. The employees who went through the learning process pass on what they have learned to their colleagues using the workshop method.

Diffusing knowledge

Regardless of the knowledge infrastructure that you put in place, you need to encourage and facilitate the diffusion of knowledge so that there is a willingness to share and learn among your organization's workforce.

There are several strategies you can use for promoting knowledge diffusion. You should provide incentives to share, promote a culture of trust and collaboration, and tailor information to individuals.

The first strategy, providing incentives for employees to share information, involves encouraging employees who take part in the knowledge-building process to distribute this knowledge when they return to their departments or units. It's of no benefit to an organization if all the skills and knowledge are localized in a single area.

Incentives are used to encourage employees to contribute to the learning infrastructure. For example, you could create a system that records entries that employees make to knowledge databases or internal information systems. The more valid entries that are made, the more credits an individual receives.

Another way to incentivize employees is to put in place a system for evaluating stored information. The more useful the information is, the greater the reward the person receives.

For example, Ross is a manager of a search engine optimization, or SEO, company. He creates an internal information system for employees to contribute to.

Ross receives an e-mail notification each time an employee adds information to the system. At the end of each year, rewards are given based on how frequently an individual uploads new, relevant information.

The company's employees are made aware of the bonus system when they start. They also know that the quality of the information they contribute is more important than the frequency of their contributions. This prevents employees from making irrelevant entries solely for the purpose of qualifying for the bonus.

Question

Which statement about providing incentives to share information is correct?

Options:

1. Companies reward employees based on the number of knowledge contributions they make

2. Companies reward employees based on the number of relevant knowledge contributions they share

3. Companies reward employees based on the number of times they access an internal information system

Answer:

Option 1: This option is incorrect. Companies reward employees based on the number of relevant knowledge contributions they make. This prevents irrelevant contributions being made by employees just to benefit from an incentive scheme.

Option 2: This is the correct option. Employees are rewarded for contributing knowledge that's relevant to the company, and that benefits other employees.

Option 3: This option is incorrect. Companies reward employees based on the amount of relevant knowledge contributions they share. Simply accessing a knowledge information system isn't the same as contributing to it. Companies value and reward employees who contribute and share information.

The second strategy for diffusing knowledge is to promote a culture of trust and collaboration. People have to work hard to gain knowledge and they'll be willing to share it only if they feel that others are also contributing. As a leader, you should try to create an environment where people actively want to share information.

You can achieve this by running regular group activities. Ensure that there's inclusive participation and mutual respect between group members. Encourage the group to communicate freely without worrying about company hierarchies. This will encourage participants to offer frank and insightful observations and to be willing to receive feedback in return.

In your role as a leader, you should lead by example. Don't be afraid to discuss mistakes that you've made. This will allow you to outline what knowledge you needed to build to correct your errors.

Remember Ross, the manager of the SEO company? He decides to organize a group discussion. He asks members from different departments to attend.

Developing a Culture of Learning

Several attendees have recently completed training in areas identified by a learning needs assessment. Ross wants the entire group to benefit from this newly acquired knowledge.

Ross begins the discussion by inviting one of the attendees, Beth, to discuss the training she recently received in pay-per-click techniques. After she finishes, he asks the rest of the group if they think they can apply what they've learned from Beth to their own roles.

The third strategy for promoting knowledge diffusion in an organization is to tailor information to individuals. This involves giving employees some control over how they receive, process, and integrate information. You can use specific software programs to create individual user profiles for each employee. As information is contributed to the organization's databases or internal information system, the software program identifies what items may be of use to each user based on the criteria they have outlined.

Consider again the example of Ross and the SEO company. He commissioned a software program that acts as a filter for all the information that's flowing into the company's internal information system.

Employees set the specific criteria for their own user profiles. This means that information relating to their role is accessible from their desktop.

The company has different clients from a range of industries. Ross creates industry-specific teams to work with clients in that industry. Each team member can set criteria such that information relating to a certain industry immediately comes to that person's attention.

Question

Which examples may contribute to the diffusion of knowledge throughout an organization?

Options:

1. A manager of a commercial marine biology research company creates a reward system to encourage employees to share information

2. A manager of a health and safety firm uses group-based activities to encourage the workforce to collaborate

3. A sales manager of a clothing web site creates individual user profiles for members of the sales team

4. A manager of a vehicle rental company asks employees to provide yearly reports about learning initiatives they have been involved in

5. An owner of a publishing company uses a software encryption program to make sure only senior management can access the company's databases

Answer:

Option 1: This option is correct. A reward system provides an incentive for employees to contribute and share relevant information.

Option 2: This option is correct. Group-based activities are an ideal method for promoting a culture of trust and collaboration.

Option 3: This option is correct. Creating individual user profiles for employees is a way of tailoring information to individuals. This approach gives employees some control over how they receive, process, and integrate information.

Option 4: This option is incorrect. Providing yearly reports about learning initiatives won't help diffuse information through an organization. The diffusion of information should be a regular, continual process. Yearly reports are an ineffective way to diffuse information.

Option 5: This option is incorrect. Only allowing senior management to access information is an ineffective way to diffuse information.

Applying knowledge

Applying knowledge is the fourth practice relating to organizational learning. The learning initiatives that an organization carries out will be judged on how effective and how useful they prove to be. As soon as knowledge is built within the organization, it must be used to modify behavior and performance. For instance, if training was given to address a production problem but the problem persists, the training was ineffective.

Three of the most effective strategies for applying knowledge are to provide opportunities to practice, to use learning as the basis for new action plans, and to reward the use of knowledge and insight. Ideally, these strategies are used at the same time.

Providing opportunities for employees to practice what they're learning is a highly effective way of applying knowledge. You should create a simulated or real environment for trainees to conduct practice sessions.

Developing a Culture of Learning

These sessions require trainees to solve problems using their new skills or knowledge.

You can increase the level of practice by allowing trainees to carry out unsupervised practice. You then give them feedback based on their results. As they progress, you can vary the practice exercises until each trainee achieves the required level of competence.

For example, Lori is a manager with a company that provides financial auditing support. She's responsible for the company's training program. She provides the trainees with sample audit problems based on real problems the company has encountered. She then provides the trainees with feedback regarding their progress.

Using learning as the basis for new action plans is another strategy for applying knowledge. This involves identifying new methods, procedures, and techniques that your employees have learned about and translating them into actions.

If new and better methods for carrying out tasks are identified during a learning initiative, these methods should be tried out. As well as applying knowledge, this approach will help to drive initiative and efficiency in the organization.

For instance, Lori identifies an effective technique that streamlines the process of creating financial statements. She recommends that this process become part of the company's standard operating procedure in the future.

Question

Match each example of applying knowledge to its corresponding strategy. Each strategy may have more than one match.

Options:

A. A biochemical engineer uses a new testing procedure under simulated conditions

B. A metal fabricator receives feedback about how he used a new technique

C. An IT support company creates a new standard operating procedure because of a training outcome

D. An e-marketing company incorporates a new function into its service offering because of a need identified in a training initiative

Targets:
1. Providing opportunities to practice
2. Use learning as the basis for new action plans

Answer:
Carrying out tests under simulated conditions and receiving feedback about the use of new techniques are examples of providing opportunities to practice.

Creating new operating procedures and incorporating new functions as a result of training are examples of using learning as the basis for new action plans.

The third strategy you can use for applying knowledge is to reward the use of knowledge and insight where it enables increased problem-solving skills or helps generate new opportunities for the organization. By providing incentives and recognition for employees to apply newly acquired knowledge, you're helping to create a learning culture. You'll find that members of your workforce will return from learning and training initiatives with new ideas. When these prove to be beneficial, the person should be rewarded.

Remember Lori, the manager with a company that provides financial auditing support? Lori wants to encourage her colleagues to apply the knowledge they've acquired from learning initiatives and training.

She rewards members of the workforce who suggest ideas that will benefit the company. Travis is a member of the company's public sector audit team. He recently completed training in how public sector organizations can increase the transparency of their auditing process.

He suggests to Lori that he can prepare a briefing session for his colleagues because the skills he has acquired can also be applied to private industry. Lori recognizes the value of Travis' contribution. She personally thanks him and tells him that she'll put a positive note in his personnel file.

Question

Jeff is the manager of a telecommunications company. The company has introduced several practices to support learning initiatives. As a result, Jeff issues a directive requiring that all training programs enable learners to put their skills to use in real and simulated environments. He also creates a merit scheme that acknowledges contributions from employees that will benefit the company.

What combination of strategies for applying knowledge does Jeff use to promote long-term changes based on learning?

Options:

1. Providing opportunities to practice and using learning as the basis for new action plans

2. Using learning as the basis for new action plans and rewarding the use of knowledge and insight

3. Providing opportunities to practice and rewarding the use of knowledge and insight

Answer:

Option 1: This option is incorrect. Jeff does provide opportunities to practice strategy, but he doesn't use learning as the basis for new action plans.

Option 2: This option is incorrect. Jeff does reward the use of knowledge and insight but he doesn't use learning as the basis for new action plans.

Option 3: This is the correct option. Jeff uses a combination of strategies that provide opportunities to practice and reward the use of knowledge and insight.

In addition to providing opportunities to practice and rewarding the use of knowledge and insight, Jeff should have created new action plans for the company based on the new methods, procedures, and techniques that his employees learned about.

CHAPTER FOUR
Evaluating and Sustaining Organizational Learning

Creating an ongoing learning culture

Good health is never the result of a one-off event, but rather a case of continual upkeep. Similarly, an organization's health is based on continuous learning. Successful organizations know it's a process, not an event – one that keeps up with the latest developments, information, and trends.

Organizations and their employees must always be actively learning. A sales representative needs to learn about a new product, while an IT worker needs to know about software updates. These actions are promoted in an organization-wide learning culture.

Organizational leaders should notice several paradigm shifts as an effective learning culture develops. For example, employees may go from competing with one another to collaborating. A company may also change from having a local focus to a global one.

Where once manager-driven initiatives may have been the norm, employee empowerment may have taken over.

A rigid or procedural working culture may develop into a flexible one. Organizational leaders should encourage these paradigm shifts.

If a learning culture isn't nurtured in an organization, it may fade into complacency about improvement.

As learning becomes institutionalized, members of the organization are expected to continually learn new behaviors, attitudes, and skills.

Regression back to previous behavior is likely if a learning culture isn't actively sustained.

Sustaining a learning culture

There are four strategies for sustaining a learning culture within an organization: reinforce, reflect, renew, and review and report.

The first strategy for sustaining a learning culture is to reinforce it. To help achieve this, provide an infrastructure for learning. This helps ensure learning opportunities are maintained. A learning infrastructure typically requires strong knowledge management practices and optimal use of information technology.

A learning culture can be reinforced by fostering the application of learning in on-the-job contexts. It's also reinforced through experimentation, collaboration, and systemic thinking where employees build new understandings by working with complex situations or subjects.

Egalitarian relationships help pave the way for collaboration and open communication in the organization, which strengthen the learning culture.

Developing a Culture of Learning

Above all, personal motivation for learning is key and should be constantly encouraged.

Promoting good practices also reinforces the learning culture. This is helpful in areas such as planning for knowledge gains, building knowledge, diffusing knowledge, and applying knowledge.

It's particularly important to keep tight alignment between your learning efforts and the strategies and operations of the organization. This alignment makes it easier to show how learning is meeting business needs. An advisory learning council within your company can help oversee the alignment between learning and organizational strategy, to ensure that learning activities are directly linked to business goals.

Take the example of an electronics manufacturer where production line employees have regular lessons on fabrication techniques. This is part of an organizational strategy to speed up production methods. However, the lessons soon become repetitive and stop improving production times. The company's advisory learning council spots this issue and adjusts the training to make it realign to the original company goal.

Question

The responsibility for reinforcing a learning culture should be delegated to an advisory learning council in the organization.

Is this statement true or false?

Options:
1. False
2. True

Answer:

Option 1: This statement is false. This isn't the only tool to help reinforce a learning culture. Others include providing the infrastructure for learning and encouraging collaboration amongst employees.

Option 2: This statement is not true. Several other tools help reinforce a learning culture. Everyone in the organization, including employees themselves, should bear some responsibility for sustaining a learning culture.

To reflect – the second strategy for sustaining a learning culture – refers to learning about learning. One reflection technique is to use learning histories.

- Document facts from various learning processes to help you understand their benefits, and learn about best practices and theories in the field of learning.
- Find out what other organizations are doing to build their learning cultures.
- Network with successful companies, and discover their approaches to learning.

Take the example of Juan, a training manager for an online advertising organization. He's trying to improve the standard of the company's search engine optimization, or SEO, with a training program. He looks back at previous programs and reviews participant questionnaires.

The questionnaire's results indicate that technical aspects of the program are beneficial. However, some participants said the program was unfocused. Juan tackles this issue by studying best practices regarding SEO programs.

He researches similar SEO programs from other organizations, in addition to studying instructional design theory.

Developing a Culture of Learning

Question

Which action is an example of the reflect strategy of sustaining a learning culture within an organization?

Options:

1. Kieran promotes the practice of applying the knowledge gained from his recent IT lecture to his team's regular working day

2. Kieran looks back over a successful lecture on IT to understand why it was so well received by those in attendance

Answer:

Option 1: This answer is incorrect. This is an example of another strategy for sustaining learning and a learning culture, reinforcing knowledge.

Option 2: This answer is correct. Trying to understand why a lecture was successful is an example of "learning about learning" from history.

Renewing a learning culture is the third strategy for sustaining it. Test, challenge, and question existing knowledge and practices periodically. Such processes help ensure that knowledge gained from learning doesn't become out of date.

If you have stored knowledge from previous learning experiences, add to it as necessary. Databases full of knowledge can stagnate if left alone.

Use various tools to build and refine your knowledge base. These tools might include workshops in business awareness or scenario planning.

Self-evaluation and dialogue sessions also help to constantly update the foundation of your organization's learning culture.

To review and report is the fourth strategy for sustaining an organization's learning culture. The two components go hand-in-hand. First review the learning efforts to make sure learning is taking place, and that it's effective in bringing about change. Then report the results to communicate your findings.

For example, a gaming hardware company begins lectures for its engineers on market trends. The regular lectures aim to help the engineers, who work in the Product Development Department, improve their interaction with the Marketing Department.

Participants are regularly surveyed on how helpful and applicable these lectures are. These surveys focus on collaboration levels between the Product Development and Marketing Departments.

Each lecture is reviewed using the surveys and its effectiveness is reported on. The results of the reviews are available to everyone in the company.

Question

What are examples of managers implementing strategies to sustain a learning culture within their organization?

Options:

1. Alan meets with a successful management counterpart to compare learning cultures

2. Stephanie challenges whether existing IT guidelines within her company are up to date

3. Edgar informs his employees of a health and safety lecture that might be of interest to them

4. Michael relays information on whether induction training for his interns was valuable to his CEO

Developing a Culture of Learning

5. Lionel uses a piece of information from his travel company's presentations database to prepare for a speech to employees

6. Claire sits on a learning advisory council that ensures her film company's production training links to the company's annual strategy

Answer:

Option 1: This option is correct. Alan is employing the reflect strategy, in which he can learn about learning by exploring best practices from other organizations.

Option 2: This option is correct. Stephanie is employing the renew strategy. Questioning whether guidelines are up to date prompts investigation and renewal of them if necessary.

Option 3: This option is incorrect. While Edgar's initiative will be part of his company's learning culture, the action itself won't help sustain it.

Option 4: This option is correct. Michael is employing the review and report strategy. Relaying the results of the training's effectiveness shows it was worthwhile.

Option 5: This option is incorrect. While Lionel is utilizing information, he's not adding to or renewing the database.

Option 6: This option is correct. Putting in place an advisory council for this purpose is an example of the reinforce strategy.

Importance of evaluating learning

Many people across the world regularly contribute money to savings funds and check to make sure they're getting a return on this investment. Businesses who invest in learning face the same issue. As they put money into educating their workforce, they want a return on any learning investment. To make sure this happens, learning activities should be evaluated.

Evaluating the success of a learning activity is important for several reasons. It proves its worth and encourages buy-in from key stakeholders in the organization. Just as important, it motivates people to participate in learning activities.

Today's business climate demands that every part of an organization proves its worth. As such, this is the first reason why it's important to evaluate learning efforts. Demonstrating the impact of learning on your business justifies your investment in it.

Developing a Culture of Learning

Next to payroll, a company's largest investment in people is learning and development. This strategic investment boosts the intellectual capital of employees.

A workforce's business knowledge, skill sets, attitudes, motivation, and adaptability together form its intellectual capital. Each of these contributes to producing financial capital for an organization and influences market value.

Evaluation of intellectual capital is helped by employing various financial and nonfinancial metrics. There are several highly technical methods for measuring these metrics, such as targeted testing, but there's no universal format.

Take the example of Anne, a financial director with a large insurance firm. The organization invested $4,000 in an IT Department network infrastructure training program. Anne must ensure this investment proves its worth.

Her evaluation reveals that security changes in the organization's data back-up infrastructure, which was a training program objective, saved the organization thousands of dollars. These changes saw data being backed up instantly in a separate data center. Previous methodologies were more costly and time-consuming.

Question

Carlos is an HR manager with a data center which recently provided employee training programs on new time-logging software and updates to older security technologies. Carlos is evaluating the success of the training.

How can this evaluation process help prove the worth of the training program?

Options:

1. It can help Carlos judge if new time-logging and security technology was needed
2. It can help Carlos prove that it was strategically important for the company to invest in the training
3. It can help Carlos to introduce the idea of intellectual capital as an economic resource within the company
4. It can help Carlos introduce other training programs to his superiors

Answer:

Option 1: This option is incorrect. The reasons why the new technology was needed should be ascertained before the training begins.

Option 2: This option is correct. Carlos' evaluation may prove that the training has increased the capabilities of the organization.

Option 3: This option is correct. In his evaluation Carlos can prove that it's been economically beneficial to increase the knowledge and skills of employees.

Option 4: This option is incorrect. His evaluation will concentrate on the benefits to the company. Introducing the need for more training is irrelevant at this point.

An organization's key stakeholders always need to be convinced their investments and efforts are sound. This is why the second reason to evaluate learning activities is encouraging buy-in from these leaders. Evaluation helps highlight how continued learning adds value to an organization. It helps convince stakeholders they should support learning initiatives.

Knowledge is one of the most important resources for any organization. As with any valuable asset, key stakeholders should be aware of how that knowledge is being managed.

Developing a Culture of Learning

Remember Anne, the financial director with a large insurance firm? Key stakeholders in her organization have questioned how much the company has spent on learning initiatives. However, Anne points toward the value of a recent training program on social networking for the Marketing Department.

Her evaluation shows that many valuable new customers attribute their allegiance to the organization's improved social media presence. Convinced by Anne's evaluation, the stakeholders approve more spending on learning activities that are projected to help grow the company's customer base.

Motivating people to participate is the third reason it's important to evaluate learning activities. Employees are more likely to engage in learning if they understand how it benefits them and the company.

When leaders show employees how learning new behaviors, approaches, skills, and attitudes helps improve company performance, learning becomes institutionalized into the company's culture.

Fostering a culture of continuous improvement of a company's learning culture will benefit employees. Valuable personal development can be found within these new behaviors, approaches, skills, and attitudes.

For example, Anne is currently preparing a learning seminar for the Finance Department on legislation.

Her evaluation of previous seminars noted that attendees benefited from open discussion of skill levels, leading to improvements in employee confidence. Anne shares her older evaluation results with the Finance Department, emphasizing the benefits of the new seminar.

She informs them that the company stakeholders are dedicated to evaluating the benefits of the legislation seminar as well. This encourages Finance Department members to pay more attention to its possibilities.

Question

Which managerial actions are examples of motivating people to participate in learning?

Options:

1. A CEO places evaluating learning amongst her top priorities for the year ahead

2. A training coordinator observes newly hired IT employees to see if they have a different approach than established employees

3. A manager emphasizes to his sales team that improved sales techniques often lead to improved profits and commissions

4. A sales manager creates a questionnaire on attitudes to learning for his team

Answer:

Option 1: This option is correct. When leaders of an organization believe learning is a priority, employees are encouraged to take part.

Option 2: This option is incorrect. This action doesn't motivate established or new employees to learn.

Option 3: This option is correct. This is an example of showing how learning can be of personal benefit to employees and to the organization as a whole.

Option 4: This option is incorrect. This is unlikely to play a role in motivating the sales manager's team to take part in.

Difficulties of evaluating learning

There are two common difficulties you'll face when evaluating learning: determining the causes of change, and determining the financial return on learning – which is particularly challenging because learning has many intangible benefits.

When it comes to human behavior, it's notoriously challenging to pinpoint the causes of change. New behavior may be the result of learning initiatives, or it may be caused by personality traits, recent experiences, or other influences. Because evaluating learning involves evaluating people, you have to be aware of the different factors that can influence people's behavior.

Take the example of Jennifer and Kevin, who are physical therapists. They work with a private medical company and both recently took part in a training program on back exercises. Kevin felt the program was worthwhile and begins using specific exercises from the training program. His supervisor correctly noted that this was the result of the training.

Jennifer felt the program was outdated. After studying alternative back exercises in her spare time, she alters her methodologies as well. Her supervisor notices this but, unaware of the real reason for it, attributes it to the training program.

The second difficulty to arise when evaluating learning is identifying a financial return. Financial benefits of learning can be hard to quantify. For instance, an employee who participates in software training may feel better prepared to handle the complexities of designing or maintaining a data backup system. However, it can be difficult to measure how this newly bolstered knowledge helps the company in terms of returning the financial investment in the training itself.

Learning objectives and baselines

Successful organizations reinforce their learning culture through a series of learning and development activities. These include knowledge-sharing schemes, creative collaborations, training programs, self- directed learning programs, seminars, and many other activities.

To ensure all these learning opportunities are of benefit, evaluate them. Make sure that people are actually learning, and that learning results in changed behaviors or attitudes. Ultimately, it must also improve the organization's bottom line. Evaluation of learning activities must assess not only the impact on the individual, but also how this translates into observable benefits for the organization.

You may have said that determining objectives was a key step to take before a learning activity even begins. This step helps to ensure a robust evaluation process afterwards. Another important early step is determining baseline levels of knowledge or performance.

See each action to learn more about it.

Determining objectives of learning activity

Determining objectives for a learning activity guides your evaluation by highlighting what the activity must achieve. With the help of relevant stakeholders, set out what impact you want the learning activity to have on both the individual and the organization.

Determining baselines

Measuring what people know and what they don't know in advance of a learning event gives you a baseline to compare with their knowledge and performance after the learning event. The impact of learning is often easiest to assess if the baseline reveals a specific issue to overcome.

For example, Grace is sales manager for a telecommunications organization selling tablet PCs. Customers recently complained about her team's product knowledge.

In response, Grace creates a training program on the subject. The main objective of the program is for the sales team to understand the technology involved in their tablet PCs.

To set baselines that will ultimately help determine whether or not the program achieved its objective, Grace uses questionnaires. Her team members answer questions on their company's product. Grace will administer similar questionnaires after the program finishes, comparing the later results with the baselines to determine whether product knowledge has improved.

Question

How do setting objectives and measuring baselines help you evaluate learning?

Developing a Culture of Learning

Options:

1. This process helps set out what participants are expected learn from a learning activity
2. This process helps you to quantify the monetary benefits of a learning activity
3. This process makes it easier to note differences in employees after a learning activity
4. This process helps demonstrate desired operational changes after training
5. This process helps document skill levels of employees before training
6. This process allows you to rectify errors in training before it begins

Answer:

Option 1: This option is correct. Setting out what participants are expected to learn helps to outline distinct objectives for the employees in question.

Option 2: This option is incorrect. This process takes place when looking for the return on investment of a learning activity.

Option 3: This option is correct. Simplifying matters to help see the differences in employee performance after a learning activity is an advantage of determining baselines.

Option 4: This option is correct. Finalizing desired operational changes is an advantage of determining objectives of learning activity. Targets are therefore set for the organizational impact expected after training.

Option 5: This option is correct. Documenting the skill levels of employees before training takes place is an advantage of determining baselines. It allows you to view where your company's knowledge levels are.

Option 6: This option is incorrect. Setting baselines and objectives looks into what will happen after training. This process isn't concerned with focusing on retrievable errors in the training itself.

Levels of learning evaluation

Many organizations use the Kirkpatrick Model to evaluate their learning activities. Dr. Donald Kirkpatrick reasoned that the effectiveness of training can be divided into four levels: reaction, learning, behavior, and results.

The first level of the Kirkpatrick Model, reaction, establishes a participant's response to the learning activity. The next level, learning, assesses whether participants have improved their knowledge, increased their skills, or changed their attitudes through the learning activity.

Behavior is Kirkpatrick's third level. Having taken part in learning, do participants apply the knowledge gained from it in their work? Has it changed their behavior?

Finally, the results level assesses whether the desired organizational outcomes of the learning activity have been achieved.

Many learning experts recommend a series of questions that evaluate learning activities in a way that roughly parallels Kirkpatrick's levels: how did employees respond to the training? What did participants learn? What was the effect on performance? What was the impact on the organization? And what was the return on investment?

See each question to find out more about its importance.

How did employees respond to the training?

Asking how participants responded to training begins the evaluation. Decipher whether it was a positive or negative experience for them.

What did participants learn?

With learning objectives established, asking what exactly did participants learn helps ascertain whether those targets were met.

What was the effect on performance?

Asking what was the effect on performance helps illuminate the impact of learning on a person's work practices.

What was the impact on the organization?

Take the focus away from the individual and ask how the learning has benefited the organization as a whole.

What was the return on investment?

Finally, ask what was the return on investment? This is essentially an extension of the question about organizational impact, this time expressed in monetary terms.

The five questions on successful learning move increasingly outward. Beginning with the individual, the questions build progressively toward the effect on the entire organization. This topic will focus on the first three questions, regarding reaction, learning, and performance. The other questions will be covered elsewhere in the course.

Developing a Culture of Learning

Question

Sequence the questions on the success of a training program.

Options:

A. What was the impact of learning on the organization?
B. What was the effect of learning on performance?
C. How did employees respond to the training?
D. What was the ROI?
E. What did participants learn from their experience?

Answer:

How did employees respond to the training? is ranked - This question is asked first to give an initial insight into the success of the learning activity. Positive reactions indicate that training may result in valuable results for the individual.

What did participants learn from their experience? is ranked - This question is asked second to move the evaluation toward the training's actual value. It helps you begin to see if a training program has met its objectives.

What was the effect of learning on performance? is ranked - This question is asked third to allow you to assess how learning has been applied, asking if the knowledge gained helped someone's work performance.

What was the impact of learning on the organization? is ranked - This question is asked fourth to establish how learning has affected the organization as a whole.

What was the ROI? is ranked - This question is asked fifth to help show the financial bottom line of the training program. It measures how much money was gained or lost through the training program.

Assessing reactions

Each of the five questions used to evaluate training has its complexities. You must examine them closer to understand them. First you should focus your attention on how employees responded to training.

You can use surveys and other tools to gauge employee response to a learning activity.

Or you can use interviews and group meetings to get a more detailed reaction from participants.

These tools can ask participants whether the learning activity was of benefit to them, and whether it met its intended objectives. Participants must give honest answers in both interviews and surveys for this assessment to be useful.

Due to the array of responses possible when asking someone's reaction to training, intangible benefits may come to light. For instance, interviews or surveys could uncover a sense of increased commitment to the organization.

Developing a Culture of Learning

Participants may react positively to training, though it doesn't always mean they've learned anything. This is why getting someone's response to training is only one part of a larger assessment picture.

However, if responses are positive, it suggests that employees were open to learning from the activity. If responses were negative, this might suggest that they're not open to learning, or that the activity itself was ineffective.

Take the example of Simone, laboratory manager with a medical devices company. The organization's lab workers recently participated in health and safety training. Simone used group meetings to elicit their reactions to the training sessions. There was a positive reaction to the training structure, and several lab workers mentioned how training emphasized their importance to the company, which they found motivating.

Question

Positive reactions to learning events indicate that participants have met the learning objectives from the event. Is this statement true or false?

Options:
1. False
2. True

Answer:

Option 1: This statement is false. While positive reactions indicate participants reacted well to learning, they don't indicate that the desired objectives were actually met.

Option 2: This statement is not true. In order to ascertain whether the desired objectives of the learning activity have been met, more questions have to be asked.

Assessing learning

The second question to ask in an evaluation of training is what did participants learn? This question is based around objectives and baselines, which are used to compare what should have been learned and what's actually been learned.

Following any learning activity, you can use a number of tools to evaluate what participants learned. These tools help collect data on what learners have gained from the experience. They include objective tests, performance tests or simulations, case studies, and exercises, all of which are typically integrated into the learning activity itself.

See each assessment tool to learn more about it.

Objective tests

Objective tests are based around precise responses, which are either right or wrong. Usually true or false, multiple choice, or matching questions, they're easy to score.

Performance tests or simulations

Performance tests or simulations offer participants the chance to demonstrate what they've learned. Tests and simulations should be modeled upon the content of the training.

Case studies

Case studies are detailed descriptions of a relevant problem or situation, followed by several questions about it.

Exercises

During exercises, what participants learned during training is explored, reviewed, and scored. Some exercises involve problem solving, and others involve participants practicing skills gained from training.

Remember Simone? She's assessing what learning resulted from her lab workers' recent health and safety training program.

She asks lab workers to complete a simulation of five different safety procedures which were part of the program.

Using this assessment, Simone finds that workers struggle to complete two of the five simulations, both of which concern fire safety. This indicates that both of these procedures need to be better explained during future training.

Question

Match the appropriate evaluation tools with the questions they relate to. Each question may have more than one match.

Options:

A. Multiple choice tests on training content
B. Group meetings for training participants

C. Case studies with questions related to the training topic

D. Surveys on the quality of training

Targets:

1. What did participants learn?
2. How did employees respond to the training?

Answer:

Multiple choice tests and case studies with questions that relate to the training topic help ascertain what participants learned from a learning activity. Both offer measures of what knowledge or skills have been gained from a learning activity.

Group meetings for training participants and surveys on the quality of training are both methods of finding out how employees responded to a learning activity. Both offer forums for participants to give an honest opinion on the training.

Assessing performance

Having assessed both reaction and learning, the third question to ask during an evaluation process is what was the effect on performance? Use this question to judge whether someone's work performance has changed, improved, or evolved due to learning.

The effect learning has on performance tells you whether behaviors have changed in line with expectations.

Quantitative measures of this progress are desired if possible. For instance, learning may result in fewer errors or more sales by an employee.

This crucial part of evaluating a learning activity reiterates the importance of setting objectives and baselines. Performance levels should reach decided-upon objectives. Knowledge of pre-learning performance baselines helps you identify the changes that occurred.

Several methods help detect performance changes. Action plans are effective – both in terms of setting targets and tracking a participant's progress in meeting them.

Structured interviews can also be utilized, as specific lines of questioning help evaluate effects on performance. Similarly, appraisals of performance also help monitor the effects of learning, as can observation of the participant's performance.

Performance changes can also be evident in rising or decreasing error rates from a participant in a learning activity. Falling or increasing complaint rates involving that participant can also indicate performance changes. The use of new tools and procedures by those who have participated in a learning activity can also indicate changes in performance.

Simone used a simulation of five different safety procedures to find out what workers learned from a health and safety training program. Three months on, she evaluates whether this new knowledge has affected performance.

Lab workers' performance in the simulation indicated they learned new guidelines to help decrease safety procedure error rates.

After the simulations, Simone put in place a team-based action plan to track if this would happen. Under the plan, a 5% decrease in error rates is expected each month. Simone discovers this target has been met each month.

Question

Match the appropriate evaluation tools with the questions they relate to. Questions may have more than one match.

Options:

A. Presenting a training-related simulation

B. Recording error rates or complaints prior to training

C. Discussing participants' impressions of a learning activity in a group meeting

D. Observing the effects of training on an employee

E. Holding structured interviews with those who took part in training

Targets:

1. What was the effect on performance?
2. What did participants learn?
3. How did employees respond to training?

Answer:

Recording error rates or complaints prior to training allows you to measure a reduction in them following it. Observing the effects on an employee following training is a simple way to monitor if it was worthwhile. Holding structured interviews allows you to ask direct questions on the effect training has had on participants. All of these strategies measure the effect on performance.

Placing participants in a simulated situation can reveal what they've absorbed from a given learning activity.

A group meeting is a useful tool for ascertaining employee responses to learning events. An open discussion amongst participants can reveal if they view the activity in a positive light.

As you evaluate the effects learning has on performance, unanticipated results and outcomes may arise. This could mean changes in behavior, attitude, demeanor, or even altered work processes. These performance-related outcomes can have significant benefits. Unexpected performance shortfalls can even be enlightening. Organizations with a learning culture embrace the information from these shortfalls as opportunities to learn.

Case Study: Question 1 of 3
Scenario

As an HR manager for a pharmaceutical company, Isabelle is currently evaluating the success of a legislation training program for the Research and Development Department. The in-house program was two days long including lectures and a final exam.

Having circulated reaction sheets to the research and development team, she's received a generally negative response. Recurring complaints were that the course was repetitive and at times irrelevant.

Answer the questions on the evaluation process for the legislation training program in the given order.

Question

What can Isabelle conclude from employee reactions to the legislation training program?

Options:

1. The level of complaints suggests that the program may not be on the right track

2. The research and development team may not have been open to learning from the program

3. The complaints point toward a lack of commitment to their job from the research and development team

4. The current course structure has no benefit to the research and development workers taking it

5. The reaction to the training program reflects an intangible benefit for the organization

Answer:

Option 1: This option is correct. Repetitiveness and irrelevant elements of the program require closer examination.

Option 2: This option is correct. A negative response to training can indicate that the team wasn't open to training. This reaction is only a small piece of a larger picture regarding the evaluation of a learning activity.

Option 3: This option is incorrect. The research and development team's negativity doesn't point toward a lack of commitment to their jobs, just a poor impression of the training.

Option 4: This option is incorrect. While the research and development team pointed to some repetitiveness and irrelevant sections, they didn't say it was of no use.

Option 5: This option is incorrect. While employee responses to learning activities may hint at intangible benefits for the organization, such as increased satisfaction or commitment, the poor reaction in this case is not evidence of such benefits.

Case Study: Question 2 of 3

What actions could Isabelle take to perform the second level of evaluation for the training program?

Options:

1. She can ask participants if their commitment to their jobs has been increased through the program

2. She can ask participants to take part in a simulated exercise which reflects the legislative lessons from the program

3. She can present the participants with a set of questions on legislation taught in the course

4. She can compare the baseline knowledge of the participants with their knowledge levels after the program

5. She can present a questionnaire to employees on how helpful the training program was

Answer:

Option 1: This option is incorrect. Questions about commitment fit into the first stage of questioning – gauging participant reaction to the program. But even at that stage, Isabelle is likely to probe commitment subtly, rather than asking about it directly.

Option 2: This option is correct. A simulated exercise can indicate whether the program's intended lessons were taken on board.

Option 3: This option is correct. Using a set of objective questions, Isabelle can quickly establish what knowledge has been gained from the program.

Option 4: This option is correct. Before the program began, the organization will have determined what level of knowledge the participants had. This can be compared with what's been learned after the program.

Option 5: This option is incorrect. This question belongs to the part of the evaluation concerned with the participants' reaction to the program.

Case Study: Question 3 of 3

What actions could Isabelle take to perform the third level of evaluation for the training program?

Options:

1. She can hold structured interviews with the team on how they are applying legislative principles in their work

2. She can hold a group meeting with the team to reinforce what's been learned from the program

3. She can compare the baseline legislative error rates for the team before and after the program

4. She can compare baseline numbers for legislation-related mistakes against the targeted reductions in the program

5. She can observe the team at work to see if there are any delays related to legislative research

Answer:

Option 1: This option is correct. By carefully planning the contents of these interviews Isabelle can ascertain if performance has changed.

Option 2: This option is incorrect. This type of group meeting will only go over what was learned in the program, rather than how the knowledge has been applied.

Option 3: This option is correct. Error rates provide a quantifiable measure of changes in performance.

Option 4: This option is incorrect. Isabelle should be comparing baseline figures with actual results.

Option 5: This option is correct. Observation of work is one of the recommended tools to use when trying to ascertain changes in performance.

How learning impacts the organization

An evaluation of a learning experience focuses on the individual first. While this is key to measuring the effectiveness of learning, organizational stakeholders are likely to be more interested in determining the impact of learning on the organization, including the return on investment, or ROI.

Evaluating the impact of a learning activity on an organization concerns direct changes. For instance, organizations can undergo significant cultural changes such as better teamwork, reduced absenteeism, or greater employee satisfaction. Other, more easily quantifiable changes include increased production rates or sales, a decrease in mistakes, or higher profits.

When an organization invests in learning, leaders expect to see the impact of that learning.

This level of assessment is primarily concerned with business metrics – the quantifiable components of the organization's performance.

Developing a Culture of Learning

Common business metrics include error rates, complaints, staff turnover, customer feedback, wastage, financial turnover, accident rates, or trend line analysis.

Question

In what ways can an investment in learning impact an organization?

Options:

1. Increased production rates
2. Increased employee satisfaction
3. Improved customer feedback
4. Decreased level of staff turnover
5. Improved employee knowledge levels

Answer:

Option 1: This option is correct. As employees implement knowledge gained in a learning activity, production rates should improve.

Option 2: This option is incorrect. Though it may eventually benefit the organization, this is an individual-level benefit, not an organizational one.

Option 3: This option is correct. Learning can result in better customer service, leading to better feedback from customers.

Option 4: This option is correct. Learning activities geared toward improving employees can boost job satisfaction, helping keep employees on board.

Option 5: This option is incorrect. This effect of learning refers to the individuals themselves, rather than the organization.

Tangible benefits of learning

Whether the benefits of learning are tangible or intangible, their impact takes time to become apparent. It may take a while for employees to transfer their learning into real world situations.

Before any learning activity takes place, establish specific projections for its success in business terms. These targets are based on the content of the learning activity and will align with the organization's business strategy.

After a sufficient amount of time, evaluate if these projections have been met. Using quantifiable measures, compare actual results with the original projections.

Quantifiable measures are easiest to work with because they return numerical data for effects that can be counted or measured. Qualitative measures, on the other hand, return verbal descriptions of effects. These descriptions are usually imprecise and difficult to compare with other measures.

Benefits of learning will either be tangible or intangible. Tangible benefits often relate to monetary measures or production figures.

Intangible benefits are related to less concrete areas like enhanced reputation, accountability, or clarity.

Tangibles always prove easier to quantify than intangibles. However, it's possible to quantify many intangibles using various methodologies.

Common tangible elements include speed of product development, productivity, and employee retention.

See each tangible benefit for more information about it.

Speed of product development

Speed of product development typically refers to product rollout speed. As lessons are learned from training, production may run faster than before.

Productivity

Productivity is based around discovering whether employees who take part in a learning activity are more productive than those who don't. This could relate to areas like greater production numbers, more sales, or decreased error rates for example.

Employee retention

Following a learning activity, you may investigate whether it resulted in fewer employees leaving and lower employee turnover costs compared with previous time periods.

Take the example of Aiden, HR manager of a smartphone manufacturer. He's evaluating the success of a product development training program for the organization's design team. The program took place after a product launch and as a new development began. Aiden waits until the smartphone resulting from that development is released six months later to do the evaluation.

Aiden initially looked for improvements regarding productivity. Compared to pretraining levels, he found the design team reported a massively reduced error rate in this production process. As a result, time previously assigned to fixing errors could be devoted to product development instead.

Also, compared to previous product development periods, employee retention increased dramatically. Previously, employee retention levels had been poor during development, often delaying the process. The design team also halved the time it took for their product development duties, meaning more product testing could take place.

Quantifying intangible benefits

As well as evaluating tangible benefits, organizations need to evaluate the intangible benefits of learning activities. Intangibles include qualitative paradigm shifts such as a transition to a flatter hierarchy, a shift from rigid procedures to more flexible ones, or a move from competition to collaboration on teams.

You may have noted that you can use scoring methods to quantify intangible benefits. For instance, customer satisfaction can be measured numerically using customer satisfaction scores. You may also have noted that you can measure an intangible benefit by breaking it down into its component measurable parts.

Consider an intangible benefit such as a paradigm shift from management-driven to employee- empowered decision making. The components that could be measured include employee accountability,
management responsibilities, and communication levels.

The employee accountability component could then be measured using a simple scoring system. Using scores from one to ten, employees and management mark how much they feel employee accountability has increased since a learning activity. This process can be repeated for management responsibilities and manager-employee communication levels.

Learning has a variety of intangible benefits, and most can be divided into quantifiable parts. Take, for example, innovation or marketplace agility.

See each intangible benefit for more information about how to break it into component parts.

Innovation

Innovation is difficult to quantify, however it's a valuable asset for any organization. Discovering levels of innovation gained from a learning experience isn't impossible though. For instance, a production manager with a software developer is evaluating the success of an innovation seminar for employees. The effect the seminar had on innovation is measured by breaking it into three component parts: the value and number of new products created, new patents obtained, and new services developed.

Marketplace agility

Agility in the marketplace is beneficial to any organization, but how can it be quantified? Consider Xavi's situation, for example. He wants to measure the gains in agility that result from his research team completing a marketing training program. In his evaluation, he splits agility in the marketplace into two quantifiable parts. First he measures the average time between deciding on an idea and the product arriving on shelves. Then he measures response times for altering products following test-based feedback.

Question

Which examples describe effective ways to assess the organizational impact of learning?

Options:

1. Morten's HR Department takes a legislation seminar and he asks what effect it'll have on their performance

2. Two months after his IT team attends a software seminar, Charles evaluates its effects on software error rates

3. After Jemima's sales team takes part in a sales innovation seminar, she measures the impact of innovation with a question and answer session

4. Miguel's sales team takes part in a motivation seminar, and he does an assessment of its impact two days later

5. Denise's IT Department does an accountability training program, and then she measures the results the following year by examining employee responsibility and employee-management communication

Answer:

Option 1: This option is incorrect. Morten's line of questioning focuses on the individuals in his HR Department rather than the organization.

Option 2: This option is correct. Charles is giving ample time for the lessons of the seminar to sink in with his IT team. He's also focusing on business metrics rather than individual ones or performance ones.

Option 3: This option is incorrect. Jemima should break down innovation into component parts before trying to measure it objectively.

Option 4: This option is incorrect. The organizational results of training will take time to be noticed, so this is far too soon for Miguel to carry out his assessment.

Option 5: This option is correct. Denise's decision to split the evaluation of accountability into parts helps measure an intangible benefit.

Return on learning investment

The final question in the evaluation of a learning activity is often the most complex to answer: what is the return on investment, or ROI? Essentially an extension of the previous question about organizational impact, it measures how valuable the learning initiative has been in monetary terms.

ROI is about dollars spent versus dollars gained, or costs versus returns. It seeks to determine whether the financial investment in training has been worth it.

So to calculate the ROI, you need to convert the benefits of learning into monetary values.

Why is ROI so important? Because it's a chief concern of those at the highest level in the organization. CEOs, chief financial officers, and senior management take interest in the financial benefits of any learning activity.

For example, Peter is the HR manager with an audio equipment manufacturer. He's assessing the success of a manufacturing productivity training initiative for employees.

The learning initiative was expected to improve production speed by 30% over the course of a year. Having spent $54,000 to create and make time for the training program, the company's senior management wants a favorable ROI.

As production speed increases, it takes seven months for this to turn into a $80,000 net profit increase in comparable figures from the previous year. The initiative has led to financial gains that exceeded the investment.

To calculate ROI, you divide net cash benefits by net costs, and multiply by 100. See each element of the ROI equation for more information about it.

Net cash benefits

Quantified and expressed in terms of dollars, net cash benefits can come in the form of revenues or savings made from increased production, decreased errors, or improved efficiency levels.

Net costs

Quantified and expressed in terms of dollars, net costs will include the cost of arranging the learning activity, the loss of working hours for the employees involved, and funding the evaluation process.

x 100

ROI is typically expressed as a percentage, so you multiply the ratio by 100.

A positive ROI means that benefits exceed costs, which is the aim of any learning initiative. The greater the ROI, the greater the financial value. Note that it often takes time for a learning activity to produce a positive ROI, and that ROI can increase over time as new benefits are realized.

Rita manages an aesthetics company, which invested $6,000 in sending its aestheticians to a customer satisfaction seminar to increase repeat customers. Rita's training program evaluation notes that after one year, the number of repeat customers increased by 30%, translating into net benefits of $41,000. Rita divided $41,000 net cash benefits by $6,000 net costs. This gave her the result of 6.83, which she multiplied by 100 to give an ROI of 683%.

Question

A small GPS technology company invests $2,000 in an innovative time management course for employees. This also involves losing $700 worth of working hours. The course results in a new product prototype being ready for investors far more quickly than previous prototypes. Before the product is even picked up by investors, this improved time has meant savings of $4,000 in working hours.

What is the ROI for the building company from the training program in those six months? The answer is to be given as a percentage.

Answer:
1. 148.1%
2. 148%
3. 148.1
4. 148

The limits of ROI

Though it may be favored by financial decision makers, the ROI alone is inadequate for evaluating the success of a learning activity for two main reasons. First, there are many unintended, value-added results which arise from learning activities. Second, the volume of intangibles complicates matters.

Because people benefit from learning in different ways, a learning activity can result in some unexpected advantages. When evaluating a learning activity, these benefits are called unintended value-added results.

Take the example of a sales-focused training program expected to result in increased sales and revenue for a consumer electronics organization. While sales and revenue increased after the course, there was also a dramatic rise in customer satisfaction.

Note that while an ROI assessment may be able to take into account customer satisfaction if it's measured, it may be unable to take all unintended value-added results into account.

Unintended value-added results are sometimes discovered during the evaluation process. As you observe the results of learning, differences in employee performance become noticeable, or attitude changes come to light in feedback collected from questionnaires. If a benefit was unanticipated, you probably didn't collect baseline data prior to the training initiative, so you may not have firm comparative data to incorporate into the ROI calculation.

Remember Peter, the HR manager with an audio equipment manufacturer? He's assessing the success of a manufacturing productivity training initiative for employees.

The course was expected to improve production speed by 30% over the course of a year. A year later, that target has been met. However, Peter also conducts interviews with employees on the program's impact on their work.

The interviews show many unintended value-added results. Employee feedback confirms improvements in teamwork and employee accountability. Meanwhile the program also encouraged additional innovation in production methodologies.

Question

ROI assessments don't have to cover unintended value-added results of learning as they're outside the purview of ROI.

Is this statement true or false?

Options:
1. False
2. True

Answer:

Option 1: This statement is false. While unintended value-added benefits are difficult to quantify and include in the ROI for a learning activity, it is possible to do so. Leaving them out may lead you to underestimate the ROI.

Option 2: This statement isn't true. Unintended value-added results such as increased adaptability are difficult to predict and account for, but they should still be included in ROI where possible.

The volume of intangibles that result from learning can also be an obstacle to getting accurate ROI figures. In fact, ROI usually doesn't take into account intangible benefits because these can rarely be expressed as monetary values.

For example, if a toy company sends its designers to a product innovation program, company managers will want to evaluate if it was worthwhile. However, innovation is an intangible benefit and its effects may not be quantifiable as a dollar amount.

Sometimes you can count on expert stakeholders to assign accurate dollar values to intangibles. In the case of the toy company, the organization's chief financial officer may deem that innovation resulting from the program brought the company an extra $50,000 in revenue. This may be an estimate based solely on the observations of the chief financial officer.

Sometimes stakeholders can't assign monetary value to intangibles though. In such cases, the intangible benefit should remain as it is. It should be reported separate from ROI, in a qualitative manner.

Question

Developing a Culture of Learning

Deborah is the training manager for a public relations company. She's evaluating the ROI of an Entertainment Department orientation to project management. The goal of the orientation program is to increase job satisfaction.

Match each element of Deborah's evaluation with the category that describes it. Each category may have more than one match.

Options:

A. Deborah determines that ROI was only 20% after six months

B. Deborah's structured interviews reveal the program improved communication levels

C. Deborah notices job satisfaction doubled according to questionnaires

D. Deborah learned that client satisfaction rates increased following the orientation

E. Deborah's questionnaires reveal job satisfaction is easily assessed by employees now

Targets:

1. Projected tangible benefit
2. Unintended value-added tangible benefit
3. Unintended value-added intangible benefit
4. Cost

Answer:

Deborah's discovery of raised job satisfaction rates and increased knowledge of job satisfaction amongst employees would be projected tangible benefits from the orientation.

Deborah's discovery that client satisfaction rates had increased is an example of unintended value- added tangible benefits.

Deborah's structured interviews, which reveled improved communication levels, are an example of an unintended value-added intangible benefit.

Deborah's process of determining the ROI is an example of evaluating the cost of the training program.

REFERENCES

References
1. **Organization Development: A Jossey-Bass Reader** - 2006, Joan V. Gallos (ed), Jossey-Bass
2. **Building the Learning Organization: Mastering the 5 Elements for Corporate Learning (2nd Ed)** - 2002, Michael J. Marquardt, Davies-Black Publishing
3. **Winning Decisions: Getting it Right the First Time Winning Decisions: Getting it Right the First Time** - 2002, J. Edward Russo and Paul J. H. Schoemaker, The Doubleday Publishing Group
4. **How to Manage Training: Facilitating Workplace Learning for High Performance** - 2007, Carolyn Nilson
5. **Handbook of Organizational Learning and Knowledge** - 2001, Meinolf Dierkes, Oxford University Press
6. **Workplace Learning and Development: Delivering Competitive Advantage for**

Your Organization - 2007, Jackie Clifford and Sara Thorpe, Kogan Page

7. **The Value of Learning: How Organizations Capture Value and ROI and Translate Them into Support, Improvement, and Funds -** 2007, Patricia Pulliam Phillips and Jack J. Phillips, Pfeiffer

GLOSSARY

Glossary

A

absenteeism - A pattern of habitual absence from working duties.

action plan - A sequence of steps that must be taken, or activities that must be performed well, for a strategy to succeed.

autonomy - Independence or freedom of thought or action.

B

baseline - A clearly defined starting point from which improvements can be measured.

best practice - A method or technique which consistently yields results superior to those achieved through other means.

brainstorming - The act of generating ideas, often performed in team settings.

C

case study - A detailed study of a person, department, or organization which focuses on factors contributing to the subject's success or failure.

CEO - Acronym for CEO, the highest-ranking executive in an organization. The CEO is responsible for executing policies set out by the board of directors.

chief executive officer - See CEO.

collaboration - The act of people working together to achieve a common goal.

corporate culture - The shared values, goals, assumptions, or norms that dictate how people within an organization interact, as well as the overall atmosphere of the organization.

cross-fertilization - The use of information from one department or team within an organization to help create knowledge in other departments.

D

data center - A centralized repository, either physical or virtual and designed for continuous use by several users, which is equipped with hardware, software, power conditioning, and data backup technology.

database - A collection of data organized such that it can be quickly stored or retrieved.

E

egalitarianism - The promotion of power sharing, participation, and responsibility at all levels of seniority within an organization.

empathy - The ability to feel and understand the concerns of others.

evaluation - The act of analyzing the quality or worth of something.

F

feedback - An evaluative response from someone which gives information regarding the result of a process or activity.

H

hierarchy - A ranking of people of different seniorities.

hindsight - Recognizing the outcomes of an event after its occurrence.

HR - See human resources.

human resources - Abbreviated as HR, the department within an organization that's focused on activities relating to employees, including orientation and training of current employees, employee benefits, and retention.

I

inertia - The tendency for things to remain unchanged.

infrastructure - The underlying structures, either physical or organizational, required to operate a business or organization.

institutionalized - The process of integrating fundamental values and objectives into the organization's culture and structure.

intangible - Something generally considered ill-suited to being assessed or measured because it has no physical substance – for example, company good will.

intellectual capital - Collective term for the value of an organization's employee knowledge and business training, and any proprietary information which provides the company with a competitive advantage.

K

Kirkpatrick model - An evaluation model based on four levels of evaluation: reaction, learning, behavior, and results.

knowledge networks - Technology-supported repositories of organizational expertise and information.

L

learning - The continuous acquisition or modification of knowledge, skills, understanding, or behavior.

learning culture - A reflection of the beliefs and practices in an organization that encourage continuous development.

learning labs - A managerial approach that provides employees with an opportunity to simulate some of the ideas they are developing.

legislation - The enactments of a legislator or legislative body.

M

metrics - Types of measurement used to gauge quantifiable components of a company's performance.

motivation - The urge to achieve a desired goal.

N

network infrastructure - The architecture, in terms of equipment and connectivity, which makes up an organization's network.

O

objective test - A test which consists of factual questions requiring short answers that can be quickly and unambiguously scored.

organizational culture - See corporate culture.

organizational learning - Improved employee competence gained through continuous improvement.

organizational silo - An informal organizational structure that occurs when functional units work in isolation without considering the effect their actions have on the rest of the organization.

P

paradigm shift - A radical change in underlying beliefs or theory within an organization.

procedure - A set of established actions, methods, or operations for conducting the affairs of an organization consistently over time.

productivity - A measure of the efficiency of a person or system in converting inputs into useful outputs.

Q

qualitative - In research, a method of collecting information that focuses on questions of "why" and "how." Qualitative research delves into human behavior and the reasoning behind individual decision making.

quantitative - In research, a method of collecting information that focuses on questions of "who," "what," and "when," which have clear and empirically-based answers. Quantitative data is derived from statistical and mathematical modeling.

R

return on investment - Abbreviated as ROI, the ratio of capital gained or lost in relation to the amount invested. This is generally expressed as a percentage.

ROI - See return on investment.

S

simulation - An imitation of the behavior of a certain situation or process carried out by representing key characteristics or behaviors of that situation or process.

skill set - Particular skills needed to accomplish a specific task or perform a certain function.

staff turnover - The number of permanent employees who leave an organization within a reported period versus the number of active permanent employees on the last day of the previously reported period.

stakeholder - An individual, group, or business with a vested interest in the success of an organization.

T

tangible - An asset that has measurable or quantifiable properties.

W

wastage - Goods or materials which are lost as a result of breakage, decay, leakage, or shrinkage.

www.ingramcontent.com/pod-product-compliance
Lightning Source LLC
Chambersburg PA
CBHW021547200526
45163CB00016B/2574